ONE FOR THE ROAD

Julian Davison

ONE FOR THE ROAD
AND OTHER STORIES

TOPOGRAPHICA
SINGAPORE

TOPOGRAPHICA
◆

23 Bright Hill Crescent
SINGAPORE 579684
topographica@pacific.net.sg

One For The Road
— Julian Davison —
Third Edition

Printed in Singapore by Saik Wah Press

ISBN 981-04-4791-4

For A.M.D.

(who was never struck by lightning again)

These pieces first appeared as a series of articles in the Expat magazine. I would like to thank the editor, my good friend, Mr. Nigel Simmonds, who encouraged me to contribute to the magazine in the first place, and then gave me a completely free hand to write more or less what I pleased so long as it had a vaguely Singaporean connection — the authors of incidental journalism are rarely so fortunate to have such an indulgent and considerate editor.

I am no less grateful to the inestimable Helen West who read through each and every one of these pieces in all their various draft forms as well as the final versions. This was an even more arduous task than might at first be imagined for she had heard a great many of the stories countless times before. As ever, her critical comments and encouragement have been much appreciated.

CONTENTS

FOREWORD

Somerset Maugham, in *The Summing Up*, famously remarked, "There is an impression abroad that everyone has it in him to write one book," before adding dryly, "but if by this is implied a good book the impression is false." As far as the present offering is concerned, in the midst of this ragtag miscellany of autobiographical sketches, potted histories, anecdotes and descriptive vignettes, there are probably several much better books struggling to get out — a volume of childhood reminiscences perhaps, a travel book, maybe even a dissertation on some aspect of South East Asian history. But life is short and one's attentions easily diverted, and these other books may never get to be written. So, for the time being at least, these modest fragments will have to stand in their place.

Actually, writing about oneself — and I tend to figure quite a lot in these pieces — is an extremely immodest exercise if only because it rests on the inflated presumption that other people may actually be interested in learning more about one than they already know. This being so, it is customary for the man who is about to embark upon such an enterprise to begin with a few words of self-effacement or otherwise apologise for having the temerity to thrust himself forward in such a manner. "Bah, humbug," as Scrooge would have said.

So why does one write, sheer egoism aside? Well of course there is the financial remuneration, slender though this may be, for as Dr. Johnson put it, "No man but a blockhead ever wrote, except for money." But having said that, I must admit that it gave me great pleasure to sit down and think hard about my childhood and other distant places of the mind in order to put together some of the more autobiographical pieces. Although I have a pretty good memory, I have always been troubled by the idea that one day these recollections of long ago might be lost or simply fade away. Not to be able to remember the past is a terrible thing; quite apart from depriving one of the enjoyment (and sometimes the sadness) that looking back may bring, it also diminishes one's own sense of self — the amnesiac has not only lost his mind, but also his identity. I am therefore relieved to have got some of these childhood *aperçus* down on paper at last, before Alzheimer's or apoplexy can lay claim to them. As for the other stories that appear here: some were commissioned, others are about subjects that I am interested in, and some are simply about ideas or issues that happened to have caught my eye at the time that I was writing about them. I hope that they will interest and entertain the reader as they have me and if they raise the occasional smile along the way, then so much the better.

Julian Davison
Singapore, September 2001

ONE FOR THE ROAD

So, step by step, the Junior came to terms with Asia and its ways. He learned to sprinkle his conversation with Anglo-Malay argot; to talk about makan *for his food or meals,* barang *for his luggage or property,* gaji *for his pay,* chop *for his company's trade-mark.*

— Charles Allen, *Tales from the South China Seas* (1983) —

❖

Satu empat jalan"— "One four the road" — said the red-faced Englishman, and ordered himself another beer. It is less than twenty-five years since the last of the Empire-builders sailed over the horizon and into the history books. My parents belonged to that generation and although the boundaries of contemporary political correctness do not allow much room for manoeuvre here, I have to say that neither they, nor their friends and colleagues, were the rapacious villains that might sometimes be supposed from the rhetoric of post-colonial discourse. This book is intended neither as a celebration of the colonial era nor an apology for its existence. The British Empire, like my parents, was an historical fact and the Singapore and Malaysia that are recalled in the following pages inevitably reflect something of the way things were back then. And if a certain element of nostalgia for a vanished age seeps in at the corners, well that's pretty much in the nature of things. To borrow a line from Byron: "The 'good old times' — all times when old are good — are gone."

Singapore in the fifties was a very different place from today. The tallest building in town was the Deco-style Bank of China on the south bank of the river, and this early high-rise, together with the Cathay Building at the junction of Orchard Road and Bras Basah, constituted the modern face of Singapore. The crumbling shophouses and crowded streets of Chinatown, on the other hand, looked much the same as in Conrad's time, as did a lot of the rest of the island, which was still very green and rustic in those days. The trishaw had replaced the rickshaw in 1946, and there were modern cars and trolley buses, but the river was chock-a-block with bum boats and *sampans* and one could still see Chinese junks and Indonesian *prahu* at anchor off Collyer Quay.

The harbour was, of course, the dominant feature of downtown Singapore back then — a vast panorama of ships and sea and sky, reflecting Singapore's pre-eminence at the commercial crossroads of Asia's maritime trade. At night the twinkling lights of the ships in the roads lit up the horizon like a squadron of fireflies, while an onshore breeze brought the sound of rattling anchor chains to one's table at the old Satay Club, nearby Raffles Hotel. One was always conscious of the sea back then. Today, Singapore has become landlocked by its own reclamation schemes and the historic relationship between port and city has been sadly lost.

For the colonial and expatriate elite, this was a golden hour, a splash of late afternoon sunshine before the sun went down on the British Empire forever. In the days when land and labour were cheap, even a relatively modest income was sufficient to provide a gracious lifestyle. For the typical European family in the 1950s, this meant a house with a garden, a motor car, one or two domestic servants and a gardener. It was an easy life and though the winds of change were blowing fairly vigorously, most people affected not to notice. Englishmen still played cricket on the Padang — my father was one of them — while Somerset Maugham was far from moribund and if in town, could be expected to take a suite of rooms at the Raffles Hotel.

Of course, things were very different for the island's native-born population, many of whom were destined to a lifetime of grinding poverty with little, if any, opportunity for escape. The situation was especially bad in Chinatown where, in the 1950s and early sixties, there may have been up to half a million people living in circumstances of considerable squalor and deprivation. In those days it was not unusual for two hundred people to occupy a single shophouse and it is said that when George Coleman's Anglo-Indian mansion in Coleman Street was demolished in 1965, a thousand squatters were found to be in residence there.

Not everyone was as badly off as the inner-city poor and in relative terms, those who lived in the countryside, or beside the sea, enjoyed a reasonably comfortable lifestyle. The typical *kampong* house might not have come with a plumbed bathroom but it was light and breezy, with a verandah or porch for sitting out of an evening. There was water from the neighbourhood standpipe and kerosene lamps to light up the night, whilst DDT helped to keep the mosquitoes at bay. Rice was cheap, there were plenty of fish in the

sea, chickens scrabbled in the dirt and there were orchards and vegetable gardens everywhere. All in all, there was something to be said for a life among the fruit trees and coconut groves.

Which is not to say that everyone was delighted with the way things were. There were undercurrents of political unrest, mostly Communist inspired we were told, and from time to time, some festering local discontent ruptured the surface calm of daily life, as in the case of the Maria Hertogh race riots in December 1950. But the British Army was always there to restore order, while most Singaporeans, then as now, were more interested in making money than throwing stones. Certainly, in daily life it never seemed that there was much overt animosity towards the British, at least not as seen through the eyes of a child. On the surface, everyone appeared to be friendly enough, whatever their creed, colour or political persuasion, and if there were some who agitated vociferously for constitutional change, the majority of Singaporeans remained fairly disinterested in politics and regarded the colonial administration with acquiescent indifference. Perhaps it was felt that since eventual self-government was a foregone conclusion, it was simply a matter of letting events take their natural course.

Across the Causeway, it was a rather different story as the Malayan Emergency took its toll of expatriate rubber planters' lives, but Singapore in the 1950s, remained a haven of relative calm and stability compared to other countries in the region. Certainly, for the reasonably affluent — both Asian and European alike — life was comfortable and well-ordered and provided one didn't look too closely, it was quite possible to remain oblivious to the more unsavoury underbelly of post-war Singapore society.

For the Englishman who had been dealt the final hand in the great game of imperial ambitions, this was still the good life. He may have had to work hard to carve out a career for himself or to oil the wheels of government on the road to independence, but he also played hard and Singapore in those more relaxed and carefree days could offer a social life that was second to none. There were nightclubs and club nights, and galas and charity balls, and a lot of dancing beneath the stars in between. Which, in a roundabout sort of way, brings me to a word of explanation. Like their fellow expatriates in other parts of the world, the players who strutted across this particular stage spoke a rather peculiar form of English, with its own distinctive vocabulary of local terms and phrases. This created both a sense of camaraderie as well as serving to distinguish the 'old hands' from the 'new tics' or mere tourists — there was an element of schoolboy snobbery, based on the length of time one had spent in the East, running through both government and the private sector alike.

In the lexicon of the old Malayan hand, a drink was always a *minum* and if asked, the preference would generally be for a whiskey *ayer*, with ice, or a *stengah* (whiskey and water in equal proportions), or else a *pahit* (gin and bitters). When someone was sick, they were said to be 'a bit *sakit*' and they went to the doctor for some *ubat*; when something was broken it was *pecah* ('smashed'), a term that was used indiscriminately to refer to anything that was non-operational from a shattered vase to a sewing-machine that didn't work. Clothes for the laundry were placed in a *dhoby* basket, the housekeeping was done by the *amah* and the garden was tended by a *kebun*.

As has often been noted — usually by a disgruntled newcomer— there was also an inherent tendency to abbreviate the names of places, officialdom and government bodies to their initials. KL, PJ, PD, PS, JB, KKB, DO, ADC, SIT, PWD — the list read like a coded message and so it was to anyone straight off the boat from England. No less mysterious to the outsider were the various local idioms which peppered everyday conversation — what on earth was 'eating the wind' (*makan angin*), who were the ubiquitous 'eyes' (*mata-mata*) and what exactly did one do in a *chummery*? My personal favourite, was the Malayanisation of the expression 'One for the road,' which was rendered '*Satu empat jalan*,' the cardinal number 'four' (*empat*) being substituted for the preposition. This was the rallying cry for a generation of Englishmen in the East: the hour may have been getting late and it was almost certainly time to *balek rumah*, but for the drinking man (and there were many), there was always time for *satu empat jalan*.

BLACK AND WHITE AMAHS

*When considering their remarkable qualities, one sometimes
tends to forget that they were ordinary women from humble
origins and not super beings imbued with special powers.*

— Kenneth Gaw, *Superior Servants* (1988) —

❖

There was a time, not so very long ago, when maids did not come from Sri Lanka or the Philippines, but from China. Not that they were called 'maids' then; rather they were '*amahs*', or 'black and whites' if they were that very special breed, the Cantonese *amah*. The latter were instantly recognisable in their workday uniform which consisted of baggy black satin trousers that stopped short of the ankles, and a crisply starched white cotton *samfu* top (on high days and holidays the latter was replaced by a steely blue, watered-silk version). Their long hair, which when loose reached to the waist, was invariably done up in a tight bun, held in place by a hair net; jewellery was limited to a discrete pair of gold earrings and a bracelet made from a single piece of jade which had been placed on the wrist in childhood and could not, in adulthood, be removed. Many of these women, if not most, never married, preferring to take a vow of life-long celibacy and devotion to the families they served, rather than submit to the constraints of matrimony and the often cruel attentions of a beastly mother-in-law. Indeed, many cited 'fear of mother-in-law' as the principal reason for choosing to become *amah*s, but there was also something of a vocational nature to this sisterhood of household servants — a calling to which they brought the highest standards of professionalism and integrity. Whatever their personal motivations, there is no doubt that for a relatively brief period in the history of this region — little more than half a century, in fact — the black and white *amah* was the most excellent of household servants, very different in their ministrations, but nevertheless in every way the equal of that other legendary creature of domestic service, the English Butler.

The origins of the term *amah* have been attributed to a number of different sources. The most popular account claims that the word originated in India and at first was used in reference to a wet nurse, being a corruption of the Portuguese '*ama*', meaning a nurse. The lexicographers who compiled *An English-Chinese Dictionary*, which was published in Shanghai in 1908, preferred a Chinese origin, deriving the term from the conflation of *nai ma*, meaning 'milk-mother', again indicating a wet nurse. Other etymologies abound, some more plausible than others.

The famous black and white *amahs* of Singapore, the Malay Peninsula and Hong Kong came exclusively from Canton (Guangzhou) and the countryside roundabout, especially the rural communities that stretched along the Pearl River Delta of Guangdong Province. The women from this region were famous for being free-spirited, independently-minded and not afraid to forego the prospects of marriage — which in traditional China was often little more than a lifetime of servitude to one's in-laws — for the relative freedom of being a domestic servant. At least in the latter situation one could leave if one didn't care for one's employers, unlike a wife who was obliged to remain with her husband's family until her dying day, there being no recourse to divorce for Chinese women without the mutual consent of both families and the further approval of the state.

No doubt another significant factor here was the traditional reluctance of this region to bind the feet of their baby daughters. The relative absence of this crippling social convention, which elsewhere in Manchu China was inflicted on the female offspring of all but the poorest of families, enabled the emergence of a very uncommon type of Chinese woman — one who was physically mobile and who could thus earn her own living and was therefore not obliged by physical incapacity to rely on either a husband or her parental family to support her.

Of course, whether or not a young girl was able to realise this potential for independence and economic freedom depended very much on the family into which she was born. More than two millennia of the Confucian orthodoxies, which declared that "women are human, but lower than men" and asserted that a woman "should not be allowed any will of her own", had made the secondary, almost negligible, status of women in

China seem part of the natural order of things. Women were of little consequence, fit only for bearing sons and a lifetime of domestic servitude. In this social milieu, the birth of a baby girl was treated with dismay by other family members — an economic disaster of quantifiable magnitude. The bottom line was that while growing up the child would need to be fed and provided for, but that ultimately she would be married off into someone else's family. "It is better to raise geese than girls" was a traditional saying in some parts of China.

Daughters did, however, raise one interesting financial possibility — they could be put up for sale. The presentation of a daughter or two to a rich family to act as personal or domestic servants — *mui tsai* (literally, 'little younger sister') — in exchange for money was a common practice in nineteenth century China. Alternatively, unwanted daughters could be sold into prostitution to service the flourishing brothels of Singapore, Hong Kong and other Nanyang ports where half a century or more of exclusively male immigration had created a huge demand for women. More often than not there was little to choose between the fate of a *mui tsai* and a 'sing-song girl' on the waterfront.

This, then, was the world into which the fledgling black and white *amah* was born in the first decade of the twentieth century, a world in which female domestic servitude articulated by ties of family, either real or fictive, was the norm. Ultimately, however, it was a series of economic disasters and natural catastrophes which brought about the black and white *amah* revolution in Nanyang. The Depression of the 1920s, followed by the collapse of the silk industry in the 1930s, seriously undermined the Chinese economy, while severe droughts in 1929 and floods in 1931 brought further privations. The loss of the silk market to artificial substitutes such as rayon affected the area around Canton particularly badly. The Pearl River Delta, especially the district of Shun Tak, was famous for the quality and volume of its silk production. Most of the employees in the silk industry were women and the consequent loss of jobs meant that by the mid-1930s there were literally thousands of young Cantonese women leaving China each year in search of employment and a new life elsewhere.

Travelling deck class to Hong Kong, Singapore and other Nanyang destinations, they were met on their arrival by those who had come before them. The latter took them to a *kongsi* house — a sort of sorority of sisters-in-arms, which provided shelter and support for those just off the boat, helping them to find their feet and employment.

*Amah*s came in a variety of categories, the most prestigious being the cook *amah*, followed by the baby *amah* (also sometimes known as an *ayah*, a word which definitely has Anglo-Indian, Portuguese origins) and lastly a general household *amah* who was responsible for doing the housework and looking after the laundry or *dhoby* as it was more popularly known. Of course, not every family was affluent enough to be able to afford a retinue of servants which meant that often all these duties were performed by a single *amah*. The latter were known colloquially as a *yat keok tek*, literally a 'one-leg-kick'.

The *amah*'s day began before dawn and was not completed until the last meal had been eaten and the dishes washed and put away, which in most European households would have been around 9.30 in the evening. Generally, expatriate families were preferred to local Chinese employers despite the barriers of language, an alien cuisine, and strange customs and routines.

Time off was limited to one afternoon and an evening a week, with the *amah* expected to be back before 6 A.M. the following morning in order to have the house cleaned and the breakfast ready by the time the family awoke. Social life revolved around the *kongsi* house, which though incredibly cramped and crowded, provided the focal point in these women's lives away from the home of their employers. There they could relax, play *mah jong* and gossip with other *amah*s. Most *kongsi*s, operated a kind of time-share system with a roster of *amah*s laying claim to 'their' cubicle on different days of the week, each according to their own particular day off.

Perhaps the most outstanding characteristic about the black and white *amah* was the love and devotion they showed for the children in their care, who became the substitute sons and daughters they themselves never had. Often these feelings were reciprocated on the part of their charges, transcending differences of language, culture and race, to become life-long ties of affection and respect. The closeness of these relations were reflected by the universal use of the prefix 'Ah', before the *amah*'s name, which in Cantonese signifies familiarity or intimacy. Ah Wong, Ah Hong, Ah Fong, even Ah Ha, I remember them all, but most especially Ah Jong who was a paragon among *amah*s.

Her origins obscure, her date of birth unknown, Ah Jong would recall that as a child, her father used to hide her in the attic at night in case roving bands of brigands should call at the house and abduct her to be sold into prostitution in Nanyang. In this respect, she was fortunate to have belonged to a loving and caring family at a time when there were many who might have been quite happy to have been relieved of their unwanted daughters in this way.

Although it was considered unseemly to appear on stage, Ah Jong was at one point a movie actress: the advent of 'talkies' in the latter half of the 1920s put an end to that, for as an illiterate she could not read a script to learn her lines. Unlike many of her fellow *amah*s, Ah Jong was married at one point, but her husband died young leaving her with two small children who were fostered out. Quite when she came to Singapore was hard to determine, but by the advent of the Second World War Ah Jong was already working as an *amah* — she told the story of how after the fall of Singapore, she and other *amah*s followed their former employers to Changi Gaol, smuggling their tooth brushes and shaving kit to them through the barbed wire.

*

15

Ah Jong came to work for my family in 1959 and stayed for close on two decades. Ageless, serene and gracious, I never saw her lose her temper except when someone was trying to overcharge her at the local market. No doubt her beatific disposition was due, in part, to her traditional Buddhist upbringing, augmented by Taoist and Confucian values. Regular visits to the temple to consult the gods and ancestors were combined with an unending quest for 'lucky numbers', the need for the latter being directly linked to the anticipated purchase of a winning lottery ticket. Whenever my father bought a new motorcar, this was the occasion for great excitement — the number plate was bound to be 'lucky', though I don't recall this ever being the case. Old telephone directories were consulted regularly, like almanacs, pored over for hours on end in the hope that they would give up an auspicious sequence of numbers which would lead to an immense fortune, won at the sweepstakes.

Like most Chinese women of her generation, Ah Jong was know-ledgeable about the preparation of herbal medicines and other potions less easily classified. Some of her pharmaceutical activities were of a seasonal nature. For example, at Christmas time, my father was regularly presented with a gift of live turkeys by various building contractors who hoped to be employed by him in the following year. Quite a number of these creatures would accumulate in our garden during the run up to Christmas to be dispatched by the gardener on Christmas Eve, one destined for the festive table, the others for the Irish nuns at The Little Sisters of the Poor.

Those that went hence, however, did so without their feet, which appeared on Boxing Day strung in neat little rows on the washing line. After having been dried by the sun and otherwise exposed to the elements for an unspecified period of time, these desiccated turkey feet were ground down into a fine powder which was then incorporated in any number of home-made philtres of diverse applications.

Apart from her preparation of medicines, Ah Jong was also an expert diagnostician, though her aetiology of disease was more metaphysical than pathological in constitution. Often, though, she was closer to the mark than might have been imagined on a first appraisal of her diagnosis. For example, on one occasion, a friend of mine who had banged his knee falling down a volcano, asked Ah Jong if she could do something to bring down the swelling. After some deliberation, Ah Jong decided that superficial cuts and contusions aside, what really ailed him was the fact that he had been "bitten by a mosquito which had previously bitten a tiger." Accordingly, she prepared an odorous balm that looked and smelt for all the world like *balacan* paste, and this was liberally applied to his knee in a banana leaf poultice. The treatment, it must be said, was not especially efficacious, indeed my friend's health took a turn for the worse generally. It was not until several weeks later that a Bangladeshi doctor at Southampton General Hospital in England, finally correctly diagnosed my friend as suffering from dengue fever. In this respect, Ah Jong's folk diagnosis, if not her remedy, was right on target, for dengue is a febrile disease characterised by severe pains in the joints and muscles, and is indeed transmitted by the bite of a mosquito, though not necessarily one that has previously drawn the blood of a tiger.

Holidays usually consisted of a week's leave at Chinese New Year, but twice, in the nineteen years that she worked for my family, Ah Jong returned to China, by ship, to visit her place of birth, though her parents were long since dead. These sojourns in her ancestral village lasted for several months and Ah Jong would depart with bounteous gifts for surviving members of her family — a bicycle, sewing machine, packets of tomato and cucumber seed, and an extensive wardrobe of children's clothes that I had grown out of but which had been put away over the years for the great expedition to the village of her own childhood.

The occasion of her first visit to China was memorable on account of the mad Ah Lan who came as a replacement for the months that Ah Jong was away. Although a black and white *amah* herself, Ah Lan was an altogether different breed of woman who fried her sausages in bread crumbs. This novel and at first diverting culinary skill, eventually palled when repeated on a weekly basis and was ultimately the cause of Ah Lan's undoing. Not that the sausages were the whole story — Ah Lan smoked opium, kept chickens and was frequently absent from work — but it was her refusal to entertain the possibility of cooking sausages in any other way which led one day to an incandescent row in the kitchen with my mother and Ah Lan's abrupt departure from the scene.

Apart from the sausages, Ah Lan was also remarkable for her long hair which she would detach and hang from a nail in her room while resting during the heat of the afternoon. Many were the times I used to sneak up on the *amah*'s quarters and surreptitiously peek through the louvred windows at this disquieting accoutrement, hanging there on the wall like a Comanche scalp. I never quite caught a glimpse of Ah Lan *sans* coiffure, for her bed was so positioned that I could only see her legs and feet. I do recall, however, that when she departed after the affair of the sausages, she did so with her head wrapped up in an old singlet and 'the hair' was left behind in the heat of the moment. I can't remember what happened to it in the end, but it hung there for some time afterwards, a rather sinister, fetish-like object that not even my father, who was usually fairly sensible about these sort of things, felt inclined to remove.

Ah Jong's second visit to China had a tragic aspect to it. For years she had been sending Red-Cross parcels of dried food stuffs, packets of seed and other, much sought-after items which were unavailable in China at that time, to her son who had returned to China at some point after the War. After many months of preparation she set sail for Canton in the happy anticipation of soon being reunited with her son. However, when her ship put into harbour, she was met, not by her son as she had expected, but some other relative. "Where is my son?" she asked. "Oh, he's busy, he couldn't make it to the city, he's waiting for you at the village," was the reply. But on her arrival at the village, her son was still not there to greet her. "Oh he had to go away on business," she was told. "Don't worry, he'll be back in a few days." It was only on running into an old friend in the street, who offered Ah Jong her condolences, that she finally learnt the truth of her son's absence. Apparently, he had died some years before, but the rest of his family, who were virtual strangers to Ah Jong, had opted not to tell her in case she stopped sending the aid parcels.

Though thrifty and sparing when it came to herself, Ah Jong was naturally generous when it came to others. Whenever I returned from boarding school I knew that there would be a new pair of cotton, drawstring pyjamas with frog buttons and a Chinese epigram embroidered on the breast pocket, lying neatly folded on my bed, with a box of chocolates placed beside them. Then, at the other end of the holidays, shortly before it was time for my return to school, Ah Jong would lay on a munificent feast incorporating all my favourite local delicacies: *popiah* and fish ball soup, crispy *wan tan* with plum sauce and a huge platter of *mee goreng* decorated with spring onions, the latter standing vertically with their green stems splayed back like miniature palm trees.

What became of Ah Jong in the end? In 1979 my father retired to Spain and Ah Jong took an HDB flat in South Bridge Road together with some ex-*kongsi* cronies. But Singapore in the 1980s was not much to her liking and after a couple of years she decided to return to the land of her birth. Every so often I would receive a letter in London, written in Chinese by a literate friend or relative, which I would have translated by the proprietor of an Asian supermarket in Tooting Bec. She never mentioned what life was like in China, but always looked back to times that were long ago and far away. Then the letters stopped coming and after an uncertain period wondering whether there would ever be another I had to conclude that there would not. But I have the address still, and maybe one day I shall make a trip to the village of the ancestors to pay my final respects in the proper Confucian manner. I have no religious beliefs of my own, but somehow I feel this would be a fitting tribute to a remarkable woman and a much-loved friend.

ON THE WATERFRONT

Ships of all nations lay at anchor, a great multitude, passenger boats, tugs, lighters, tramps; and beyond, behind the break-water, you saw the crowded masts, a bare straight forest, of the native junks. In the soft light of the evening the busy scene was strangely touched with mystery, and you felt that all those vessels, their activity for the moment suspended, waited for some event of a peculiar significance.

— Somerset Maugham, 'P&O' (1926) —

❖

How many of us think of Singapore in terms of ships and sailors, a shoreline and the sea? Yet Singapore was founded on maritime trade and remains to this day one of the great harbours of the world, a name to be mentioned in the same breath as Hong Kong, Rotterdam, the Port of London and New York. Sadly, all evidence of this great seafaring tradition lies, for the most part, out of sight and out of mind, tidied away behind the closed gates of the Port of Singapore Authority. But it was not always the case. Not so very long ago, as one reached the end of Bras Basah Road and turned into Connaught Drive, one was confronted by a huge sea panorama filled with literally hundreds of ships of all descriptions riding at anchor in the roads. Dale Collins, describing the scene in the 1920s, could write:

> The flags of all the world flutter out to the breeze which comes romping in freshly from the ocean and lifts the white pennants from the dancing waves. There is never a time when a ship is not sliding in from the ocean or going to the waves. The rattle of chains make incessant music. (*Sea-tracks of the Speejacks Around the World,* 1923).

And it wasn't so different fifty years later, when it was still possible to drive from Raffles Hotel to Raffles Quay without losing sight of the sea. Today, however, the massive swathe of reclaimed land that runs from Pasir Panjang to Changi Point, has placed the ocean at one remove for most of Singapore's citizens: buffered from onshore breezes by the casuarina groves of East Coast Park, one has little sense of the city's littoral location as one hurries from air-conditioned shopping mall to MRT.

Of course, if one's place of work is prestigiously perched among the towering edifices of downtown Singapore, or one happens to be the dizzy inhabitant of one of those vertiginous condominiums with impossible names along the old East Coast Road — Eastern Lagoon, Palm Beach Gardens, Bayshore Park, and the like — then one is still party to a magnificent view of ships, sea and sky. But even here, the immediacy has been lost — the ocean is 'over there' now, not right in our midst as once was the case, when Collyer Quay bordered the Inner Harbour and the Singapore River conveyed the seaborne trade of distant nations into the very heart of the city.

It was the sea that brought Raffles to Singapore, both literally, aboard the *Indiana*, and because of the island's strategic location at the geographical centre of several key maritime trade routes in the Asian economy of the nineteenth century. The most important of these was of course the sea route between India and China, but local connections with the Moluccan spice islands, Borneo, Java, Cochin China (Vietnam) and Siam (Thailand) also played a critical role in securing the island's place as the clearing-house of the East.

Much of the trade in the early days of Singapore was seasonal in nature, being subject to the direction of the prevailing monsoon winds. The first junks from China would arrive shortly before Christmas and remain until the following June when a shift in the monsoon winds would take them back to Chinese ports — Amoy, Nanking, Swatow, Canton and other harbours along China's southern coastline. They arrived with starving immigrants from China's impoverished countryside and overpopulated cities who came looking to find their fortune in the 'Southern Ocean' (Nanyang); they returned with cargoes of opium which were paid for in silver. Native vessels from Siam and Cochin-China plied the same route, bringing sugar, rice, coconut oil and gamboge, a gum resin from which a bright yellow pigment is extracted, but which, in those days, was commonly used as a radical purgative. There was also an extensive trade between Singapore and Calcutta with East Indiamen and privately owned 'country' ships — so-called because they were built in India and manned by local crews — sailing up and down the Malacca Straits throughout the year with cargoes of Indian cotton, jute, wheat and opium, which were exchanged in Singapore for pepper and spices, sago, tin and silver dollars.

In local waters, the Borneo season lasted from May until October with boats from Brunei, Sambas and Pontianak, bringing camphor, rattans and other jungle products from the forests of the interior, together with pepper, edible bird's nests and gold. Arab dhows, laden with spices, sailed under a Dutch flag out of Batavia (today's Jakarta), the once mighty commercial centre of the Netherlands East Indies which within a few short years of the founding of Singapore had been completely eclipsed by its British rival.

Further south, Bugis schooners from the Celebes (Sulawesi) set forth from Macassar (today's Ujung Pandang) with cargoes of coffee and tortoise shell, and gold dust from Bali. The Bugis trading season lasted from July to November and their elegant vessels — part native design, part sixteenth-century Portuguese caravel — would anchor in the gentle waters of the Kallang Basin protected by the thin arm of Tanjong Rhu.

The Bugis were also responsible for supplying a locally-manufactured oil which became a popular hairstyling accessory for men, making Macassar a household name in pre-brilliantine Europe. The disagreeable marks that this unguinous dressing left on the upholstery of high-backed Victorian chairs gave rise to that most splendidly-named thing, the 'anti-macassar', whose lineal descendent still adorns the back of aeroplane seats and dentist's chairs.

It was Raffle's prescient vision of "a great commercial emporium" in the East, founded not on territorial conquest, but on trade, which brought this tremendous mercantile enterprise into being, but its earliest operations were modest enough. In the very first days of Singapore as an East India Company trading post, cargoes were simply brought ashore in the surf. This was down on Beach Road, which today is a long way from the sound of the waves that in rough weather made discharging cargoes a wet and hazardous task. Obviously this was not an ideal situation and a move was soon made to the Singapore River which rapidly became the principal place for loading and off-loading goods.

Raffles Place, or Commercial Square as it was then known, lay just behind this first manifestation of Boat Quay. Originally a low-lying piece of swampy ground, subject to inundation, the area was consolidated in 1823 with earth from a low hillock in the vicinity of Battery Road. Wharves and godowns belonging to European merchants, soon lined its western and southern shores and by 1858, when Commercial Square was renamed Raffles Place, these few square yards of former bog were well on their way to becoming the mercantile epicentre of South East Asian trade.

Land reclamation in Singapore is not a modern phenomenon and the contours of the island's coastline have changed, amoeba-like, in every decade since Raffles first stepped ashore at the mouth of the Singapore River. By end of the 1880s, Telok Ayer Bay, whose waters once lapped the southern end of Commercial Square, had been filled with spoil from the levelled Mount Wallich which formerly stood at the junction of Cecil Street and Maxwell Road. This rearrangement of the local geography provided a fine opportunity for creating an impressive waterfront and within a few years the seashore, from Raffles Quay at the southern end, to the mouth of the Singapore River, was lined with imposing buildings representing the commercial might of the major mercantile houses and shipping agencies in the Far East.

Until the advent of the commercial airliner, this was the 'face' of Singapore, the first glimpse of the metropolis after a long sea passage from distant parts. If they did not proceed directly to the wharves of Tanjong Pagar, passenger ships would drop anchor in the Inner Harbour, whose waves broke against the seawall of Collyer Quay. The rattling of chains was the signal for a flotilla of native craft to set forth from the shore, bearing fresh fruit, caged birds, pet monkeys on a chain, and several boat loads of tourist *bric-à-brac* to the new arrivals. Small boys dived for coins, while money-changers and tailors clambered aboard to offer their services — a tropical suit made to measure in half a day!

An observer of the scene, in the years before the last war, described an especially entertaining performance:

> One old man was smoking a cheroot and, time and time again, dived overboard with the red-hot end in his mouth. As he emerged from the water, he withdrew the cheroot and puffed away at it contentedly. His trick did not pass unrewarded. (Robert Foran, *Malayan Symphony, 1935)*.

One of the most exciting places along the waterfront when I was a child was Change Alley, which in those days was a dark passageway leading from Raffles Place to Collyer Quay. Tarpaulins, stretched between the buildings, created the atmosphere of an Arab *souk* and all the world East of Suez was there to greet you and assist you with your purchase, speaking in a multitude of fractured tongues and soliciting vigorously for your attention. What would Tuan care for? What would Mem like? Kalimantan gold or Kelantan silver, moonstones and opals from Nepal and Tibet, or rubies from Burma, Javanese *batik* and Indian cottons, Sumatran coffee and spices from the Moluccas, herbal medicines, aphrodisiacs and hair-restorers, cheap watches, Persian rugs or filigree brasswork from Arabia? Or how about a dirty postcard? Ferocious haggling was the order of the day, but just about anything could be bought at Change Alley, at knock-down prices, using almost any currency one cared to part with. Best of all, to my mind, were the battery-operated Japanese 'robots' made of painted tin which whirred and whizzed and flashed their lights as they lunged about in a mechanically spasmodic manner, emitting the occasional 'bleep.' Fantastic!

The Singapore River presented an altogether different kind of waterfront to Collyer Quay with its paint-blistered godowns and narrow side alleys that led to the boiling cauldron of humanity that was Chinatown. The teaming quays and crowded waters were famously a scene of colourful confusion to the casual onlooker with hundreds, perhaps thousands, of lighters, bum boats and *sampans* wedged together as tightly as sardines in a can. As it happens, the flow of river traffic was carefully regulated at strategic points along the quayside so that *twakow* (lighters) transporting goods to and from the vessels in the outer harbour could load and disburse their cargoes in an orderly fashion. This movement of river craft back and forth found a natural counterpart in the flux and ebbing of the tide. Indeed, the latter, imposed its own schedule with incoming cargoes catching the rising tide and outward bound cargoes leaving on a falling tide. Another consideration was that some of the bridges spanning the upper reaches of the river could only by negotiated at low water when the river level had fallen sufficiently to allow the passage of barges beneath them.

In those days the Singapore River was still one of the great spectacles of the East — in the 1960s some 8,000 tons of cargo moved up and down its reaches every day. Not everyone who gazed upon its oily waters was filled with admiration however. That "pestilent tidal creek", wrote Walter Harris in 1934, while a year later Robert Foran observed that crossing Cavenagh Bridge always filled him "with acute repugnance, and was made possible only by the vigorous smoking of pipe or cigarette".

Picturesque, the Singapore River may have been, but life was hard and dangerous for the boat men and stevedores whose daily sweat and backbreaking toil provided the raw ingredients for this popular postcard scene. Most of the traffic up and down the river was man-powered — the *twakow* lighters may have been able to use their sails in the open waters of the harbour, but they had to lower their masts to negotiate the bridges that spanned the river — and in these turbid waters they were propelled by oar, or otherwise punted upstream with poles. This was pretty strenuous work and though in later years tug boats were employed to speed things up, it was not until the early 1970s that a new generation of fully motorised 100-ton lighters were introduced.

But if the *twakow* men had a tough time of it, their lot in life was a relatively easy one compared to the men who loaded and off-loaded their cargoes. These were the *chor coolies* — literally 'rough labourers' in Hokkien, by which was meant the very lowest of the low, men who laboured in ragged sweat-stained clothes beneath a blazing sun, humping their heavy loads along narrow gangplanks stretched between *twakow* and quay side. Rice and sugar came in 100-kilogramme sacks, cement was a trifling 60-kilo bag. For these men, the working day was long and arduous, the remuneration paltry.

Tuberculosis was an occupational hazard while the river itself was an open sewer — in the 1970s there were an estimated 21,000 squatter habitations lining the banks of the river between Read Bridge and Ord Bridge. Clearly there was no way that such a state of affairs could be allowed to persist and the past quarter of a century has seen the river transformed as Singapore and her citizens have been rigorously subjected to the Procrustean rack of Progress.

And so, today, the godowns and the old riparian import and export businesses have all closed, the *twakow* have been relocated, along with the sea, and the Singapore River is just a decorative basin of water to be glanced at drunkenly from the bars of Boat Quay. Great things are promised us when the current redevelopment of the riverside is completed — a glut of new hotels, yet more shopping arcades, and a spew of ersatz Mediterranean restaurants to be added to the Mickey Mouse pleasures of Clarke Quay. But the tide is out, the boats are gone, and life is elsewhere, methinks.

FLYING HOME

Home. In Anglo-Indian and colonial speech this means England.
— Hobson-Jobson: The Anglo-Indian Dictionary (1886) —

❖

The first time I flew from Singapore to Kuala Lumpur, it was in an old Malayan Airways Dakota, a DC3 with twin propeller engines and a little wheel at the back which thrust the nose of the aeroplane high in the air when it was on the ground. I believe the Malayan Airways Dakotas were all decommissioned military aircraft — the sort one sees in war movies, ferrying a platoon of paratroopers into action. Certainly the interior of the aircraft made few concessions to the concept of passenger comfort and those who flew in them were provided with little more that a seat and a seat belt — no soft furnishings here.

I think we took off from Kallang Airport, though it may have been Paya Lebar, and flew north up the West Coast of Malaysia, or Malaya as we called it then. And how green it was: rubber plantations and jungle-clad hills with the occasional brown river meandering in lazy loops to the Malacca Straits. Nowadays the entire west coast of Malaysia seems to be one enormous conurbation — from the air one is hardly ever out of sight of a housing estate or an industrial park; either that or one looks down on huge, livid laterite scars where the land has been cleared for some future development. In that earlier time, however, it was conceivable that there might be tigers in the forests and crocodiles in the rivers. Nowadays the only 'tigers' to be found in these parts are economic ones and they have turned out to be paper thin; as for crocodiles — they only get to make a cameo appearance as handbags and shoes.

During the flight, I recall that there were cockroaches scuttling up and down the aisle and that a beautiful stewardess came round with a bunch of bananas, breaking one off for each passenger in turn. Later she passed around a bag of boiled sweets to help 'pop' our ears when landing; I was allowed to take a handful, the prerogative of childhood.

Of the actual visit to Kuala Lumpur itself I remember very little, except that there were double-decker buses, painted a brilliant Bugatti blue. Later, my family went to live there and it was the most charming of towns with its Moorish colonial architecture and shady streets lined with ancient rain trees, but the blue buses were sadly no more.

My first flight to England was an altogether different matter. This was going to be a big event for although I was born in London, I was whisked away to foreign climes almost as soon as the umbilical cord had been cut and I had absolutely no knowledge of the place, other than that it was populated with people called aunts and uncles and the odd grandmother or two. On this trip I was accompanying my mother while my father was to join us a few weeks later — in those days it was customary for those who lived and worked in the East to take six months' 'home leave' every two and a half years or so, and my mother had elected to go on ahead in order to find a place to rent for the duration. Not that there was much 'home' about it — my father was born in Singapore and my mother in Trieste and both of them had spent most of their lives away from England, apart from a spell in London after the War. And as for myself, well as I have indicated, my experience of England up until this time was strictly embryological.

But to get back to the flying bit, this was in the days of BOAC — British Overseas Airways Corporation, for those who may not remember — and the world's first commercial jet airliner, the de Havilland Comet 4. The Comet had an unfortunate start to its career which began with a series of horrifying and at first inexplicable in-flight crashes. It was all rather eerily like Nevil Shute's novel, *No Highway*, published a few years earlier. Later it was discovered — I think I'm right in saying this, but I must confess, I haven't checked my aviation history — that a small window in the toilet had been changed, somewhere in between design and production, from being round or oval in shape, to square. Now the sides of a rectangle under pressure are a great deal more likely to buckle than the curved contours of a circle or ellipse and it was this weakness which caused the fuselage to rupture at high altitudes leading to a sudden and catastrophic loss of pressure within the aircraft and its simultaneous disintegration in mid-flight.

I have often wondered how this small but critical alteration to the design came about and I sometimes imagine the following scenario. In the de Havilland design studios, on a Friday afternoon, an aeronautical draughtsman is working on the blueprints for the prototype of the world's first commercial jet airliner. It's getting late and he wants to leave — he has a hot date — but he can't find the stencil with holes. After rummaging around amongst all the papers and sketches on his drawing board trying to locate the errant piece of stationary, he finally thinks "Sod it! I'll draw the window square, no one will ever notice ..."

Whatever the truth of the matter, it seems that although I was of a fairly tender age at that time and not much given to reading the *Straits Times*, I had nevertheless somehow got wind of the fact that Comet aeroplanes had nasty habit of dropping out of the sky and this led to a bit of a shindig when the time came to actually board the aircraft. In those days — it must have been Paya Lebar Airport by that time — one simply walked through Immigration and out on to the concrete apron where the aeroplanes were parked right in front of the airport buildings. Anyway, I can clearly remember strolling towards this huge aircraft with its tail section looming over us, the golden BOAC emblem emblazoned against a dark blue background. It was terrifying and I flipped. I took off down the runway with a teddy bear stuffed under each arm and a cabin steward in hot pursuit. "It's going to crash, it's going to crash. We're all going to be killed," I shrieked. Not very impressive — certainly not as far as my fellow passengers were concerned, who glared at me as I was ignominiously hauled on board, arms pinioned to my sides in a bearhug, my mouth hushed by the Palm Olive hand of the steward, legs still kicking wildly. "Dreadful little boy", said one. "Quite appalling behaviour", agreed another.

Of course, when I got to London some twenty-four hours later, I didn't want to get off the aeroplane. Flying was wonderful! It was sublime! I couldn't wait to grow up and become an airline pilot. Oh, and couldn't I just stay on board the aircraft until it turned around and then trip the light fantastic all the way back to Singapore?

But I am getting ahead of myself. First there was Rangoon (two punctures and a long wait while new tyres were flown up from Singapore), then Colombo, followed by Bombay, Karachi, Baghdad, Istanbul, Rome, Düsseldorf and finally London. You can see why it took a full twenty-four hours to get from Singapore to the UK in those days. But no matter, when flying turned out to be such fun.

Colombo was a wonderful place to land at that time though my memories of the airport belong not to that particular flight but date instead from a slightly later period in my life, when I used to fly out from England for school holidays in Malaya. In those days it seemed that the flights were always scheduled so that one arrived in Sri Lanka, or Ceylon as it was called then, at around four o'clock in afternoon — that is to say, teatime. As one began one's final approach one flew low over a cobalt sea dotted with the brightly painted outrigger canoes of Singhalese fishermen. A brief glimpse of white breakers and a strip of ivory sand flashed by and then suddenly, in the last seconds before touch down, one was confronted by a fantastic spectacle — coconut palms as far as the eye could see: a great feathery carpet of waving fronds, moved by an onshore breeze and magically illumined by the golden light of a late tropical afternoon. After a long Michaelmas term of grey skies and drizzle, when the sun set well before afternoon school was over (if it made any appearance at all), it seemed that one had truly arrived in some kind of earthly paradise — the fabulous island of Serendip, as celebrated by Arab mariners of old.

The plane landed and taxied up to the airport buildings — a cluster of single-storied sheds with tiled roofs and an Art Deco control tower. The doors were thrown open and in rushed a warm tropic breeze that brought with it a wonderful fragrance of spices mixed with the salty tang of the sea — after months of living with the smell of boiled cabbage and suet pudding, one could practically taste the aromatic flavours of the East on one's tongue as one stepped down from the aircraft onto the runway.

A short walk across the concrete and there was a white picket fence with a gate set in it which opened on to an immaculate lawn where there were chairs and tables to sit at and one could order some refreshments. Naturally a pot of tea was prerequisite — what else could one do but drink tea when in Ceylon? — and this came with a slice of fruit cake and a round of cucumber sandwiches — white bread and the crusts cut off.

So there one sat, sipping tea and munching cake, gazing across the runway at the aeroplane being refuelled with a waving curtain wall of coconut palms behind. Sparrows pecked at crumbs from the white tablecloth and it was only another three-and-a-half-hours' flying time to Kuala Lumpur. The Holidays had begun!

But those memories, as I say, belong to a slightly later time. One place, however, that I do clearly recall from that first flight to England was the airport at Baghdad. This was a sort of Nissen hut affair, which in the middle of the night was lit by the harsh glare of neon lights. Outside there were date palms and a few desultory patches of coarse grass, but no camels. I had expected camels — well dromedaries, actually — but there were none to be seen "Where are the camels?" I inquired loudly, "Ssh! They've all gone to bed", I was told. Disappointing.

From Baghdad we flew to Istanbul. There I had hoped to see lofty spires and minarets with Ali Babas wafting by on magic carpets, but though I scanned every quarter of the night sky through the porthole during our descent, I saw nothing but my own face, reflected back at me. More disappointment. But I loved the glow of the blue landing lights — they have the most extraordinary luminosity, intense, but not dazzling, as if someone had managed to capture the blue halo of a naked gas flame and bottle it. Even now, on night flights, I look forward to seeing them flash past the wing tip as we touch down.

And then it was London. Dawn was breaking, a sombre grey dawn with drizzling skies as we made our approach over the city where I was born but had yet to know. The street lamps were still switched on and in the suburbs the lights of early risers twinkled here and there as we rumbled over their sleepy heads. On and on we flew over this massive slumbering metropolis, like a warplane on a bombing run. Was there no end to it? I never knew a city could be so vast. A huge river lay below, were there crocodiles beneath its opaque waters I wondered?

My mother had previously changed into a whole lot of clothes the like of which I had never seen before. This strange costume — she called it a 'suit' — had been handed to a stewardess upon boarding who obligingly hung it in a closet especially designed for that purpose. 'BOAC really takes good care of you' was the slogan in those days, and they certainly did back then. Not only did you arrive at your destination with freshly pressed clothes, but you were given a buttonhole to complete the *ensemble* — a sprig of white heather or a spray of orchids, depending on whether you were flying East or West. My mother's legs were sheathed in a curious, smooth material, which she called stockings and were those really white gloves she was pulling on? I thought only the White Rabbit wore those.

Then we were on the ground and being bundled into a bus which ferried us to the Arrivals building. I was wearing a new item of clothing myself — something called a duffel coat, which was stiff and awkward and meant that my arms no longer hung by my sides but stuck out at an angle like the stuffed limbs of a rag doll. But I liked the little wooden toggles that fastened it at the front. More astonishing, however, was the blast of icy air that hit my face as we emerged from the warm interior of the aircraft and descended the steps to the ground. The month was November, I think, and it was about six o'clock in the morning and it was raining — it seems to have been like that in England ever since. Back then, it felt like I was standing in front of an enormous refrigerator with the door open, which was the only prior knowledge of intense cold to which I could relate this novel experience. I was astounded.

My aunt Doris was there to meet us. She was kitted out very much like my mother in a suit with stockings and white gloves, but she was also wearing a fur hat which was quite striking. In those days, flying half way across the world was considered to be something rather marvellous and one got suitably dressed up for the occasion.

After an interminable wait for our luggage — I think some of it had been taken off the plane at Düsseldorf or had been sent on to Paris and we had to make a report but the missing luggage office wasn't open due to the early hour of the morning and so on and so forth — some things don't change — we queued for a taxi (one seemed to have to do a lot of waiting around in England). The taxi, which was going to take us to my aunt's flat in Battersea, was in itself a revelation, with its funny loading bay at the front for suitcases and doors that opened 'backwards' and sliding glass windows between the driver and the passenger compartment, the latter smelling richly of saddle soap and leather. A further surprise was the fact that the taxi driver was an Englishman — I'd never seen that before. What is more, he spoke in a funny voice and called my mother "Darling," which was something to reflect upon.

That first ride from Heathrow into town along the Great West Road has remained with me to this day. Everything was grey: the sky, the streets, the buildings. Even the few pedestrians who were out and about in such inclement weather seemed to be dressed all in grey and had grey faces, at least to someone accustomed to the healthy brown faces of the East. Better to have called it the Grey West Road — England was turning out to be a monochromatic country with an awful lot of rain.

And on every roof were strange, metallic, twig-like things. "They're television aerials", I was told, not that this left me much the wiser. "Like the wireless, but with pictures". "Oh, I see", I said, but I didn't really.

At this time, Doris — even at a very young age I never called my parents' siblings 'Auntie' or 'Uncle', except for Uncle Dennis who was about a hundred and one and had led a cavalry charge in the First World War — well, Doris leased an attic flat in a mansion block overlooking Battersea Park. "South of the River" was considered to be rather bohemian in those days, or *bohème* as Doris would have put it. She had worked in Paris for many years and according to my mother she had lived in an apartment where she kept two hundred pairs of shoes and as many bottles of pills, tablets and tinctures — my aunt was always a little worried about her health and extremely allergic to avocados and capsicums.

Anyway, the taxi deposited us on the pavement outside the Prince of Wales Mansions and we climbed, rather laboriously, the four storeys to Doris' flat, relaying our luggage — or at least that portion of it which had not been left in Düsseldorf or forwarded to Paris — from one landing to another. The mansion block was a late Victorian affair and had not been designed with a lift in mind. This meant that if you lived on the top floor, as did my aunt, you didn't just pop out for a pint of milk whenever the fancy took you, but rather you planned your day around a minimum requirement of descents and ascents of the grand staircase that communicated with the ground floor.

Doris' apartment was a tiny affair, tucked up under the eaves, with dormer windows that looked over Battersea Park. Trees without leaves were another amazing facet of life in England — an extraordinary idea to a someone who had only ever been previously acquainted with the vegetable superabundance of a tropical island. Of course I'd heard about winter — back in Singapore, during the monsoon season, my mother would sometimes rise from her armchair on a wet and drizzly afternoon and exclaim: "Brrr! It feels like winter; I think I'll make some scones for tea!" I hadn't quite imagined it to be like this, however. No doubt there were going to be plenty of scones for tea in the immediate future.

There was a tiny kitchen with a formica-topped table that had folding leaves which were raised and lowered at meal times, and there was a little step ladder which doubled as a stool to sit on — for some reason I was particularly intrigued by this item of furnishing. Before long, I was sitting on said stool and wolfing down a plate of baked beans on toast — fantastic — while rather less enthusiastically sipping at a pint of milk. I've never liked fresh milk much unless ameliorated by tea or coffee, but in Singapore in those days there was precious little of the stuff around — one had to go all the way to Fraser's Hill in the central highlands of Malaya to catch the merest glimpse of an udder. When I got to England, however, I found I was expected to quaff it down like there was no tomorrow. "Drink it all up, it's good for you", my mother would say, but I felt more like a goose on the way to becoming *paté de foie gras* than the living embodiment of health and efficiency.

The best thing about my aunt's apartment, however, was the bedroom. As I have said, Prince of Wales Mansions was a late Victorian pile — an eclectic *bricolage* of neo-Classical, 'Gothick' and Elizabethan bits and pieces in the manner of Norman Shaw — and Doris' *boudoir* was located in a turret, no less. The room was almost completely circular, except for where it joined the main part of the building, and it was dominated by an enormous bed, the colour and consistency of a marshmallow — well it wasn't sticky, but one sort of sank into it and it

41

was very difficult to extricate one's self subsequently. And beside the bed, there was a little round table with a Bakelite telephone — one of those old-fashioned instruments (except it wasn't old-fashioned then) which had a mouthpiece that curved round, a bit like a coal scuttle. It made a pleasant tinkling sound when there was an incoming call and of course there was none of this push button nonsense when you wanted to call out — this was a telephone that you had to dial. And because Doris had extremely long nails — rather like the carapace of cockroaches I secretly thought — she had to resort to a special dialling implement to avoid breaking these talons. This took the form of a miniature Corinthian column, in brass, and it both intrigued and amazed me. I couldn't believe that anyone would willingly disable themselves — for this is how I regarded my aunt's indulgence — in such a way that they needed the assistance of a prosthetic digit, simply in order to make a telephone call.

All of these new experiences and discoveries were by this time getting a bit much for me and suddenly the baked beans came up even faster than they had gone down — splat! — against the wall.

"Oh dear. I think it's time for a little lie down."

"Yes he's looking a bit peaky, isn't he?"

I couldn't but agree, for a wave of immense fatigue suddenly passed over me as twenty-four hours' flying time and a great deal of excitement at either end finally caught up with me. I felt myself being picked up and gently lowered onto the marshmallow bed, where I slowly sank down into its warm enveloping embrace, secured in place by feather pillows and eiderdowns. I was briefly conscious of a soft pinkish glow (the predominant colour of the wallpaper in Doris' bedchamber was a delicate shade of rose petal) and then a hushed silence, as quiet as an undertaker's parlour.

And that was how my 'first' day in England ended — an extraordinary day of novelty and enchantment. No doubt I was resuscitated at a later hour, but I have no recollection of this. No, it is my aunt Doris in her fur hat, the Great West Road, the bare trees in the park, the turreted bedroom, and last but not least, that wonderful marshmallow bed, which always come to mind whenever anyone asks me "What are your earliest recollections of England?"

THE GENTLEMAN IN STRIPES

... apart from those unfortunate animals caught in traps, which might otherwise have been sold into captivity, I have rarely shot a tiger without a pang of regret that another courageous, strong and graceful creature has died. To me they will always be the most fascinating and magnificent specimens of our Malayan wild life.

—Lieut-Col. A. Locke, *The Tigers of Trengganu* —

I was once travelling by bus along the Bukit Merah Road and happened to glance across at a fellow passenger, seated opposite. He had a distinctive appearance, being dressed in a grubby, powder-blue jacket with a Mandarin collar and a battered straw hat with the legend 'Bang Kok' crudely emblazoned in red paint around the brim. A wispy Fu Manchu moustache drooped from his upper lip, but what was truly arresting about this man was the fact that on his lap he carried the severed head of a tiger.

I stared at the tiger and the tiger stared back at me with glassy eye, like a feral Cheshire cat, except the grin was more of a snarl and the ears were flattened back in feline rage at the indignity of being thus detached from the rest of his corporeal self. The shock lay in the unexpectedness of the spectacle — like Lautréamont's meeting of a sewing machine and an umbrella on an operating table, it was the unlikely juxtaposition of savage beast (part thereof) and suburban bus, which created such a frisson of surreal surprise. But there was a time when an encounter with a tiger in Bukit Merah, or indeed in any other part of Singapore, would have occasioned more than a raised eyebrow. Rather, it would have been a vision of unspeakable horror for the hapless soul who came face to face with such a beast, for up until the end of the nineteenth century, death by tiger was literally a daily occurrence on this island, exacting a relentless toll on human life in a population that was a fraction of the size it is today.

The earliest mention of tigers in Singapore's recent history dates back to the 8th September 1831 when the *Singapore Chronicle* reported that a Chinaman had been taken on the road leading to New Harbour (Tanjong Pagar). Another unfortunate fellow was chomped nearby a short time afterwards and a couple of months later a Mr. and Mrs. Armstrong, while out for an afternoon drive in their carriage, caught sight of a tiger in the same area. Clearly the tiger was here to stay and in the next three quarters of a century, literally thousands were to lose their lives in a plague of tigers which reached epidemic proportions before the tables were finally turned, once and for all, against the 'gentleman in stripes'.

There were probably plenty of tigers on the island before 1831 — tigers are good swimmers and the narrow Johor Straits would have been trifling to them — but in the early years of the Settlement, most of the island still lay under a thick cover of primary rain forest except for the area in the immediate vicinity of the town. With so much jungle around there were sufficient deer and wild boar to feed a sizable tiger population and there was little incentive to seek out human prey. Furthermore, as George Earl observed, "... the interior of the island [was] almost unknown to Europeans", which probably explained why the presence of tigers went unnoticed. It was not until large tracts of land had been cleared for gambier and pepper farms, and later sugar and coffee plantations, that the tiger was faced with a serious depletion of his natural food resources and the hungry cats began to turn their attention to an alternative diet of human flesh.

After the 1831 incidents, there were no more sightings of tigers until 1835 — the lull before the storm, so to speak — when a tiger jumped a survey party, led by the architect, George Coleman, and broke his theodolite. On that occasion no injury was received other than to the aforementioned surveying instrument, but by the end of the decade, the situation had become a great deal more serious.

The *Singapore Free Press* in May 1839 reported that in the previous two years, human life had been taken by tigers on a regular basis and that in the past week alone, two Chinese had been killed in this way. Surgeon Edward H. Cree, writing at about the same time, mentions that "Tigers frequently carry off a coolie or two at work at the edge of the jungle [and a] reward is given by the Government for every tiger's head brought in, as they are so destructive to cattle as well as men". This tiger bounty initially stood at $20, but in July 1839, the Government upped the reward to $50 for every animal brought into town, dead or alive.

The financial inducements to take up arms against the 'gentleman in stripes' seems to have had little effect and in the 1840s, hardly a day passed without someone being slain by a tiger. A report in the *Singapore Free Press* for July 1843 provides a typical example. On this occasion, a man was killed about a mile from the Sepoy lines — first the body of his dog was discovered, then one of the man's bangles, and finally his partially devoured remains. Other human body parts were also found at the same spot from which it was estimated that altogether some ten persons had been consumed by the tiger at that place.

The death toll was particularly high amongst Chinese coolies employed on gambier and pepper farms and many plantations had to be abandoned because no one would work them. In one instance, a plantation which had been bought at $300 was later sold for a mere $25 because the predations of tigers at this particular location had been so great that no labourer could be induced to go and live there. In the end, a group of Chinese planters approached the Government and insisted that more effective action be taken against the plague of tigers, with the result that the Government increased the bounty for every tiger killed or captured from $50 to $100, and then later $150.

These high rewards encouraged a number of persons to become full time tiger hunters, especially after 1860 when the Chamber of Commerce promised a further sum of money for each tiger killed, to be added to the bounty already offered by the Government. One of the earliest of these professional tiger hunters was a French Canadian by the name of Caroll, who took up the life of a backwoods man — a kind of Singaporean Jeremiah Johnson — spending most of his time in the jungle tracking and shooting tigers. On his occasional visits to town he was instantly recognisable by his singular appearance — it was his custom to wear a large gold ring half way up his long grey beard, rather like a boy scout's toggle. Maybe the ring brought him luck, for despite the occupational hazards of his vocation, Caroll lived out his natural span and died an old man in the General Hospital.

Another professional tiger hunter was the Eurasian, Neil Martin Carnie. A native of Singapore, Carnie is described by Buckley, in his *Anecdotal History of Old Times in Singapore 1819-1867* (1902), as being a man "of a roving frame of mind, [who] never settled down to a steady life; for a time he would be the chief clerk in the Municipality, then he would become an Inspector, and then something else, but the moment he heard of a tiger his office saw him no more." Carnie would roam the jungle at night in the company of a retired sergeant major of the police force, a Malay gentleman who lived at the fifth mile on the Serangoon Road. The latter had also shot a tiger once and had found himself so well rewarded for having done so that he left the police force forthwith and set himself up as a cattle farmer, while supplementing his income as a professional tiger hunter.

A relatively safe way to capture a tiger was to dig a pit and wait for the creature to fall into it. Alfred Russell Wallace describes a tiger pit as being "shaped like an iron furnace, wider at the bottom than top, and … perhaps fifteen to twenty feet deep, so that it would be almost impossible for a person unassisted to get out of one". He adds that they were "carefully covered with sticks and leaves, and so well concealed, that in several cases I had a narrow escape from falling into them".

Not everyone was so lucky. On an earlier occasion, the *Free Press* reported that "a Chinaman, while engaged in constructing a tiger pit at the back of Mr. Balestier's sugar plantation, was pounced upon by a tiger, who after killing him and sucking the blood, walked into the jungle, leaving the body behind." The Editor dryly added: "We suppose the tiger, knowing the object of the Chinaman's labours, took the opportunity of giving a striking manifestation of his profound disapproval of all such latent and unfair methods of taking an enemy at disadvantage."

In November 1843, what came to be known as 'the first great tiger hunt' took place. Information was received that a tiger had been caught in a trap near the third mile on the Bukit Timah Road, not far from today's Botanic Gardens, and within a short while, large numbers of interested parties were making their way there. The tiger was in a pit, the mouth of which had been covered over with logs, and had evidently made several previous attempts to climb out. An eyewitness describes the ensuing events:

> There was considerable excitement, and our chief police Magistrate forgot to cap his gun; and our chief surveyor fired away his ramrod. The tiger received the first fire with sovereign contempt, the second produced a growl, and after allowing the smoke to clear, he was seen from the marks of blood to be badly wounded. As he did not move, a dapper little man thought it might be dead, and got a long bamboo, which was lying near, and gave him a prod. There was a terrible roar and a great stampede of all the sportsmen, helter-skelter through the brushwood in all directions. The tiger made a double spring at the side, and then at the mouth of the pit, and its fore claws reached to within a foot and a half of the top, when Dr. Oxley, who with Mr. Read and one or two others had stood his ground, fired both barrels down his throat and it fell back dead, never moving again.

Not much sport in that, but a year later a 'Tiger Club' was formed whose members dedicated themselves to the pursuit and dispatch of *Panthera tigris*. Their task was complicated by the difficult terrain and the thick rainforest which was quite different to the natural habitat of tigers in India, where many of these sportsmen had previously hunted. General Douglas Hamilton of the 21st Regiment of Madras Native Infantry, who was posted to Singapore in 1846, describes the interior of the island at that time as "... covered with jungle so dense that it was almost impenetrable." An enthusiast for big game hunting, Hamilton was disappointed not to be able to add a Singaporean tiger to his collection of 'heads.' He did, however, make the interesting observation that although "there was said to be a great number of tigers on the island and some

hundreds of Chinamen were reported to be killed each year by them …
as the Chinamen belonged to secret societies who were in perpetual feud
and always ready to kill each other, I am afraid that many a murder has
been falsely attributed to the 'gentleman in stripes'."

Even allowing for the nefarious activities of the Chinese triads, the
tiger problem was a serious one and there were probably far greater
numbers of deaths than were officially reported. The *Free Press*, in October
1843, commented that

> The Chinese who live in the jungle, it is known, never think of giving
> information of the ravages committed by tigers, so that it is only by
> enquiry that the facts become known. Their feelings of superstition in
> regard to tigers may perhaps be one cause of this, for we have been
> informed that they believe that when a person is killed by a tiger, his
> *hantu* or ghost becomes a slave to the beast, and attends upon it; that
> the spirit acts the part of a jackal as it were, and leads the tiger to its
> prey, and so thoroughly subservient does the poor ghost become to his
> tigerish master, that he often brings the tiger to the presence of his wife
> and children, and calmly sees them devoured before his ghostly face.

The supernatural associations surrounding tigers in both Chinese and
Malay systems of belief make interesting reading. In China, men who
lack virtue were traditionally said to become predatory man-eating tigers
when they died, while in the pre-Buddhist era, human sacrifices were
offered to malevolent tiger deities to placate them and avert their lethal
attentions. These ancient Chinese tiger gods survive today in the form of
the White Tiger Deity, Po-hu Chih-shên whose effigy can be seen in
many temples around Singapore. The latter, while conceived as a agent
of darkness, representing the negative (*yin*) aspects of nature, is also fêted
as a destroyer and expeller of ghosts and demons. In the first instance he
is feared — placatory offerings of raw pork are placed in front of his
image to avert his malign influence — while in his manifestation as a

champion against evil spirits he is ranked with the gods who wage implacable war against the legions of spectres and demons that inhabit the Chinese universe. In the latter capacity tigers are identified as a protective influence and for this reason their image is frequently found painted on the walls of temples and houses; apparently, the Cantonese make offerings to the White Tiger God at Chinese New Year in order to avert gossip and quarrels in the forthcoming year.

The Malays also have an ambivalent attitude towards tigers, recognising them as both beneficent and malevolent beings. Naturally, the tiger is feared as a wild beast of great strength and potentially lethal intentions, but on the other hand, the usual spirit-helper of the Malay shaman, or *pawang*, is the tiger-spirit, *hantu belian*. The latter is conjured up in a spirit-raising séance (*berhantu*) and is believed to enter into the shaman's body who then becomes possessed by his or her familiar. At this point, the shaman growls and scratches at the floor in the manner of a tiger and may also lick the patient's body all over, in the same way that a tigress will lick her cubs. This is the prelude to a supernatural battle between the shaman, his spirit-helper, and the malevolent spectre who has kidnapped or otherwise torments the soul of the patient.

The Malays also believe in the existence of were-tigers. Some men, especially Korinci Malays from Sumatra, it used to be said, are believed to be able to turn themselves into tigers at will. The latter can be distinguished by their unusual behaviour — for instance, they are more likely to suck the blood of their victims, vampire-style, than devour their flesh — and are greatly feared, far more so than ordinary tigers which one might encounter in the jungle. This transformation into a were-tiger typically takes place at night when the person is asleep. Sir Hugh Clifford, in his collection of Malayan stories, *In Court and Kampong* (1897), tells of a seemingly normal Malay family who subsequently turned out to be to be were-tigers. They were "quiet, well-behaved people, [who were] regular in their attendance at the mosque," and the head of the family treated his wife with great kindness and courtesy, despite her shortcomings. She for her part congratulated herself on her good fortune at having made such an agreeable match until she discovered one day that her beloved spent his nights as a were-tiger.

Whatever the supernatural dimension of Singapore's tiger pandemic in the nineteenth century, the toll of human victims was undiminished as the 1840s gave way to the 1850s. In August 1849, the *Free Press* reported that

> The attention of his Honour the Governor having been directed to the deplorable ravages committed by tigers on this island, he has expressed himself ready to adopt any measures which may tend to remove this evil. It has been suggested that persons are to be found in the vicinity of Calcutta trained for the purpose of destroying tigers, and his Honour has written to the Bengal Government requesting that half a dozen of these Shikarries should be sent to the Straits for a limited period, to be employed in the destruction of these animals. The Governor has also directed that in the meantime, should it be deemed expedient, a certain number of volunteers from the 3rd class convicts should be permitted to beat the jungle once every month, with tomtoms, horns &c., which, if they do not lead to the destruction of the tigers, may frighten them away from the island, to which they came from the neighbouring state of Johore.

As the Editor of the *Free Press* observed: "The first of these measures may probably be productive of advantage, but we should be doubtful whether the last will be of much benefit."

Tigers could appear at any time and any place, and killed with impunity. Jim Corbett, in his classic account of hunting man-eating tigers in the foot hills of the Himalayas, *Man-Eaters of Kumaon* (1944), notes that "When a tiger becomes a man-eater it loses all fear of human beings," an observation which this report in the *Singapore Free Press* of April 1851 clearly confirms:

While some Malays were collecting rattans and cutting wood in a piece of jungle near Mr. Dunman's plantation at Serangoon, they were alarmed by hearing a tiger making his approach through the underwood. They immediately commenced a retreat, but had not cleared the jungle when the tiger came up with them and singling out the fattest man in the party sprang upon him. It had dragged the body some distance ere the man's companions recovered from the fright into which they had been thrown, and pursued him with their parangs, on which the tiger dropped the body and retreated. The poor man was found in the agonies of death with his throat and face severely lacerated. The body was brought away, but the tiger, it would appear, was determined to have his meal, for the same night he carried off a Chinaman at a short distance from the scene of his morning's exploits. The Chinaman's friends on making a search found the body, with one of the legs wanting.

Harriet McDougall, wife of the Bishop of Sarawak, describes a similarly audacious attack by a tiger during a visit to Singapore in the 1850s:

two Chinamen cleared a space in the woods for a garden; but being mightily afraid of tigers, one worked while the other beat a metal drum called a gong, the noise of which they thought would scare them away. One day the working man heard the gong cease, and, looking up, he beheld man and gong both being carried off by a large tiger.

Evidently, rather than being scared away by noise, the tiger took the gong to be a summons to dinner.

In April 1851, more than thirty people were taken by tigers in the Serangoon area in a matter of weeks, while the *Free Press*, in November of that year estimated that "at least one man is taken daily on this small island." This high fatality rate was attributed to the Government's reduction of the reward for killing a tiger from $100, a few years previously, to $50 and the newspaper accordingly urged the Government to raise the reward to $150, or even $200. In the words of the Editor: "At present the loss of life caused by these ferocious animals is really shocking, and we must say that it is a disgrace to a civilized Government that more urgent measures are not adopted to put a stop to it."

But still the killing went on. In 1859 an entire village in the Bukit Timah area was abandoned after tigers had dined on several of its inhabitants, and it was no less perilous closer to the centre of town as the following account of an evening stroll along the beach indicates.

In February 1863, the German landscape artist, Eduard Hildebrandt, visited Singapore and put up at the Hotel d'Europe which once stood on the site of today's Supreme Court. One evening, after dinner, Hildebrandt decided he would go down to the beach for a postprandial breath of sea air:

The sun had gone down and the moonlight glistened in a comforting way on the ridges of the soft waves. Who could have resisted the temptation? I took off my shoes and socks, wandered further in the cool water and gathered mussels, which covered the wet sand in thousands of shapes and sizes. The uncanny nervous agitation, which is hard to overcome in high temperatures, had deserted me; I felt inexpressibly calm. Heaven only knows how far on I would have wandered, if a mangrove bush stretching out from the land into the sea had not reminded me to turn back. I took about another dozen paces when an unexpected object made me stop. Half in the shade of the mangrove, half in the moonlight, a large tiger stood before me swishing his tail. In spite of my deadly fear I noticed however that the monster was wet through and through, so had just come out of the sea. I would not be expected to describe my feelings; I only remember that on first sight my limbs became as heavy as lead, and at a stroke all the horror stories which I had ever heard about tigers came back in my memory, but that at the same time I took flight, turned as fast as lightning, and as quickly as my legs would carry me, hurried to human habitation. Only once did I look back in fear; the tiger had not followed me. He stood as before in an attitude of expectation, but in my thoughts I still now see the bright pupils of his eyes from afar.

Naturally, when he got back to the Hotel d'Europe and recounted his adventure, Hildebrandt was roundly berated by one and all for his foolishness. According to the proprietor, "Nobody who was still in possession of his five senses would take such a walk after sunset, without being accompanied by torchbearers, drum-beaters and several guns with loaded barrels."

Twenty years later, it seems that little had changed. In Joseph Conrad's story *The End of the Tether*, which is set in Singapore in the 1880s, we are told that even the areas quite close to the centre of town were "shunned by natives after business hours ... because of tigers ... coming at a loping canter ... to get a Chinese shopkeeper for supper." Then quite suddenly, towards the very end of the nineteenth century, the incidence of tiger-related deaths began to fall away sharply. I suppose the continued eradication of their natural habitat, both on the island and across the Johor Straits, had a lot to do with it, but for whatever reason the number of deaths by tiger fell dramatically in the 1890s. Even so, my grandmother, who was born in 1894 and who used to live in the last house on Serangoon Road around the turn of the century, could remember hearing the roar of tigers as she lay in bed at night.

One of most celebrated incidents involving a tiger in Singapore occurred at Raffles Hotel around the same time. It was reported in the *Straits Times* of 13th August 1902, having taken place only a few hours earlier. Apparently a captive tiger had escaped from a "native show" on Beach Road a couple of days earlier and evading recapture had found its way, not under the billiard table as popular legend would have us believe, but beneath the floor of the billiard room, which was raised off the ground on brick piers. At some point, the tiger unwisely emerged from its hideaway to terrify a bar 'boy' by poking its head through the balustrading of the verandah. The latter, when he had recovered his composure, reported the big cat to the management who sent for a Mr. Philips from the Raffles Institution across the road. The latter was abed and somewhat the worse for wear, having attended a ball at Government House only a few hours previously. Nevertheless he responded gallantly to the summons and seizing his Lee-Enfield rifle, plus a few hollow-nosed, Mark IV cartridges, hurried to the scene, still clad in his pyjamas. The *Straits Times'* correspondent described the ensuing events as follows:

> The tiger was still under the billiard room floor. There was no doubt about that; yet no amount of peering into the gloom of the under-floor region could discover his presence. Suddenly Mr. Philips saw the tiger — or thought he did. He promptly put three shots on the spot ... But unfortunately it was a brick pillar, or something similarly indifferent to rifle bullets, that Mr. Philips saw; so stalking operations were resumed. ... The noise of the three rifle shots had created some consternation, and the hotel residents soon trooped out to see what was the matter. There was no difficulty in keeping them at a distance; so Mr. Philips' movements were not impeded! At last the Shikari got a sight of the tiger; that is to say he saw his eyes gleaming in the gloom [and] Mr. Philips soon put one of those nasty hollow-nosed bullets right between the pair of eyes.

The tiger was later found to measure seven feet eight inches from the tip of his nose to the end of his tail and stood three foot four inches high at the shoulder.

Although the historian, Mary Turnbull, records that the last tiger to be shot in Singapore was at Goodwood House in 1904, there were in fact much later instances of tigers being hunted down on the island — the uncle of a friend of mine shot a tiger at Choa Chu Kang in 1928; perhaps that was the final curtain for the 'gentleman in stripes' in Singapore.

But for all the terrible ravages that tigers were responsible for in the nineteenth century, one cannot deny the magnificence of the creature and the possibility that he may become extinct, at least in the wild, in our lifetime, is a sobering thought. George Maxwell, in an evocative account of life in Malaya during the early years of the last century, writes of "the almost god-like beauty, power, activity, and strength of a tiger," and describes what it was like to go out tiger hunting on foot:

> It [the tiger] may be within a few yards of you, perhaps, seeing all that you do, itself unseen. It can steal noiselessly through the forest where you can only move with crackling of leaves and breaking twigs. You know that when the occasion comes, that wonderful lithe body can come with lightning speed through the thick-tangled growth that hampers and impedes your every movement. Finally, you know that at close quarters a man is as helpless as a child against the overpowering weight and strength of an animal that kills an ox at a blow. (*In Malay Forests*, 1907).

Maxwell, with masterly understatement, adds: "When you are on the ground following up or waiting for a tiger, you realise all this with some vividness."

That was written just over ninety years ago; today it is the tiger, not man, which is threatened with imminent extinction. Three subspecies — the Chinese tiger and its Javanese and Balinese cousins — have disappeared since 1900, and it is estimated that there may be only some 5,000 to 7,500 tigers left on the entire planet, whereas at the beginning of this century there were probably a quarter of a million in India alone. It is a sad and shocking prospect, but our generation may yet see the complete destruction of the tiger in the wild.

'O PARADISO'

If you would be happy for a week, take a wife;
if you would be happy for a month, kill your pig;
but if you would be happy for all your life, plant a garden.

— Chinese proverb —

❖

It is rare, in these modern times, to return to a place from which one has long been absent and find it virtually unchanged. It is even rarer in the case of Singapore, where nothing seems to be more than about five minutes old. Indeed, the Singapore of my childhood would be virtually unrecognisable if placed alongside today's tropical metropolis of the twenty-first century — about the only thing the two have in common is that they occupy the same geographical coordinates on the map.

Having said that, there are one or two pockets, here and there, which have managed to evade the bulldozers and cement-mixers that have so dramatically altered the face of our island home in the past quarter of a century — little lacunae in the space-time continuum where one could almost imagine that one has been transported back through the decades to the halcyon days of youth. The Botanic Gardens is one such place, especially the part in the vicinity of the main lake, which, if my memory serves me well, remains almost exactly the same as when I used to go there forty years ago.

Gardens, botanical or otherwise, are special places with a very ancient history, and almost everywhere they have been imbued with a significance which transcends the merely horticultural. In China, the First August Emperor, Qin Shihuangdi (Chin Shih Huang), celebrated his conquest of the last of the ancient feudal kingdoms in 221 B.C., by building himself a sumptuous palace surrounded by an enormous park. The latter he filled with rare animals, birds and plants collected from the length and breadth of his newly-won empire. In this instance, the royal gardens were a symbol of his imperial majesty — a metaphor for absolute domination.

Similar ideas were prevalent throughout the ancient world where no self-respecting potentate, it seems, could get by with just a palace and no palace gardens. Assyrian conquerors boasted of having cut down and extirpated the gardens of their rivals, while the Achaemenid kings of ancient Persia bragged about having planned and planted gardens of their own. The latter were described as *pairidaeza,* which in Avestan, the Indo-European language used in Zoroastrian religious texts, means an 'enclosed space'. The Greeks took over this word as *parádeisos* and the enclosed space in time came to be an 'enclosed park'. In the Septuagint translation of the Old Testament, the term was used to refer to the Garden of Eden, while early Christians subsequently took it over as a synonym for Heaven, the Abode of the Blessed Dead. The word finally entered the English language via the Latin *paradisus* and Old French, *paradis;* quite how it came to be applied to a shopping centre in Selegie Road, God only knows — a place more distant from the Garden of Heavenly Delights is hard to imagine.

W. S. Caine, on the other hand, thought that Singapore's Botanic Gardens, which he visited in 1887, or thereabouts, was

> the most delightful garden imaginable, nearer to Eden than I could have believed anything on earth to be. Here were great forest trees a mass of crimson bloom, delicate-leafed acacias forty or fifty feet high, with vermilion blossoms at the end of every twig, bushes of yellow allamanda, brilliant crotons, with ixoras, begonias, hoyas and stephanotis, blooming in the open air. (*A Trip Around the World in 1887-8*).

Caine may have been confusing his acacias with his flame of the forest, but there is no doubt that the Botanic Gardens are a place of exceptional beauty and fascination. Part of their charm lies, I think, in the underlying tensions between the wild and the domestic. On the one hand, the carefully conceived vistas, with their grassy slopes and artfully composed stands of trees, recall the English landscapes of William Kent and Capability Brown. On the other, the prospect of exotic palms, exquisitely silhouetted against the skyline together with the luxuriant tropical foliage round about, not to mention the ten acres or so of vestigial rainforest that still covers the upper portion of the gardens, informs the spectator, most assuredly, that this is not some misplaced Stowe or Chatsworth Park. Rather they belong to a very different realm of Eastern jungles, unexplored by man, in whose dark depths the tiger stalks his prey and even the angels fear to tread.

As it happens, the Botanic Gardens were indeed the "haunt of tigers" once. This was back in 1859 when a group of garden enthusiasts formed an Agri-Horticultural Society and acquired a 57-acre plot of land from one Hoo Ah Kay, better known as Whampoa, who was a great mover and shaker in the formative years of the colony and himself an enthusiastic gardener with a fabulous house and grounds along the Serangoon Road. At the time of its acquisition, the southern part of the site had previously been under cultivation, but by now had reverted to secondary forest, while the northern half was still under primary rainforest. In these circumstances, it was only natural that tigers should frequently be sighted in the vicinity.

The Gardens were initially intended simply to be ornamental pleasure gardens and the responsibility for laying them out was allocated to a man by the name of Lawrence Niven, who was a planter and the supervisor of a nearby nutmeg plantation. The first part to be developed was the area round the bandstand, which at thirty-three metres above sea level is the highest point in the Gardens. Work was completed as early as 1861 and here the genteel and the well-to-do would come, on horse or by carriage, to make their evening promenade — a favourite occupation in Victorian Singapore — while enjoying the mellifluous sounds of the brass band which regularly played at the bandstand.

The ring roads and Main Entrance came next and in 1866 excavations commenced for a lake on a newly-acquired strip of land running along the side of Tyersall Avenue. Finally, in the same year, a further twenty-five acres at the north western end of the gardens were purchased from the old Napier Estate, thus completing the original Gardens whose layout remains more or less the same today as it was nearly 135 years ago.

As I have said, in the early days the Gardens were intended more for pleasure and recreation than as a place of botanical interest and study, but in 1875 the first professionally trained botanist from Kew Gardens was dispatched to Singapore at the Government's behest to superintend the running of the Gardens. The man in question was Henry James Murton and it was he who was largely responsible for establishing the credentials of the Gardens as a place of serious scientific study and experimentation.

Murton initiated a system of plant exchanges with horticultural institutions in other parts of the world and was himself a great collector of plant specimens which he gathered during frequent field trips to the Malay Peninsula. He founded a herbarium and was also responsible for setting up the Economic Gardens in 1879. The latter was a hundred-acre site to the north of the existing Gardens, and was intended as an experimental station for the cultivation of plants with economic potential, the most famous subsequent success in this department being of course *Hevea brasiliensis*, otherwise known as rubber.

Sad to say, the true story of the advent of rubber in the Far East is much less exciting and romantic than popular mythology would have us believe. The first rubber seedlings to reach Singapore were not illegally smuggled out of Brazil by some swashbuckling horticultural hero, but actually came from Kew Gardens via Ceylon in 1877. It seems that the Royal Horticultural Society had previously received some 70,000 seeds from central Amazonia and that these had been sent with the full knowledge and acquiescence of the Government of Brazil. Only a small number of these seeds actually germinated but those that did were dispatched to various British possessions around the world in Wardian cases — a kind of portable cucumber frame. Two cases were sent to Singapore in August 1876, but though the seedlings apparently arrived here safely enough, they were left sitting in a godown for a month and by the time Murton took delivery of them, all but five had died. However, in June the following year, a further twenty-two seedlings were received from Ceylon. Nine of these were sent to the Gardens in Taiping, the oldest botanical gardens in the Malay Peninsula, and another two may have been dispatched to Durian Sabatang near Malacca. The remaining seedlings were planted here in Singapore, and most of the rubber grown in Malaysia today is descended from these very first specimens.

Despite his reforms and beneficial innovations, Murton was dismissed in 1880 — he was actually sent to prison for misappropriating $187 of the Garden's funds — and he was replaced by another Kew man by the name of Nathaniel Cantley. Cantley had previously been attached to the botanical gardens in Mauritius and he seems to have been a very systematic and well-organised man. He labelled all the plants and trees growing in the Gardens, surveyed and established the first forest reserves and was responsible for planting Malaysian timber trees in the Economic Gardens. He was also the first to promote a 'green' Singapore, with the introduction of a programme for the formal planting of trees around the city and the establishment of a civic park in the Chinese quarter of town, which sadly survives only as the name of a shopping complex — People's Park.

Cantley died in 1888 and was succeeded by a man of legendary renown, one Henry Nicholas Ridley, otherwise known as 'Mad' Ridley. Ridley came to Singapore from the botany staff of the Natural History Museum, London, and was Director of the Botanic Gardens from 1888 to 1912. He was a man of immense botanical knowledge and was fired by a missionary fervour for rubber. Not that there was anything kinky about Ridley; rather he had a vision of the future and it was covered in the sticky latex of *Hevea brasiliensis*.

On one of his early plant-collecting expeditions in the Malay Peninsula, Ridley and a British planter went out after rain and found themselves squelching their way through mud, with water almost up to their knees. As they struggled in these adverse and uncomfortable conditions, Ridley happened to make the chance remark to his companion that in South America the natives wore special boots of their own manufacture which kept their feet and legs completely dry. Evidently, the British planter thought that Ridley was completely off his rocker and it was this incident which subsequently led to the Director of the Botanic Gardens becoming known as Mad Ridley.

No doubt, Ridley's uncommon enthusiasm for rubber helped to qualify the epithet — this was in the days before the first motor cars, it must be remembered, and few could foresee the extraordinary demand for the stuff that the invention of the automobile would bring about. As it happens, John Boyd Dunlop's factory, which made the first pneumatic tyres for bicycles, had opened just a year after Ridley became the Director of the Botanic Gardens; even so, in the 1890s, Ridley's zealous promotion of rubber was still seen at best as a little 'odd,' obliging him to resort to slightly unorthodox methods in the furtherance of his cause.

One of Ridley's ploys was to slip a few rubber seeds into the pockets of visiting plantation owners — coffee and gambier were the principal commercial crops in those days — in the hope that the planters, having inadvertently carried the seeds back home with them, might then at least be tempted to give them a go. How successful this strategy was, history does not relate. In the end the turning point came with the collapse of the local coffee-growing industry in the last couple of years of the nineteenth century. This was partly due to fierce competition from Brazilian growers and the spreading disease of coffee plants which laid waste to the region's estates. Faced with an economic catastrophe, local planters were desperate enough to turn to Mad Ridley and his *Hevea* trees, and the rest, as they say, is history. By 1920, Malaya was producing more than half the world's rubber and rubber to this day continues to play a major role in the Malaysian economy. The madness of Ridley could at least be qualified as that of an idiot savant, rather than pure and simple lunacy.

Ridley was succeeded by Isaac Henry Burkhill, formerly in the employ of the Bengal Government as adviser on economic botany. The crowning achievement of Burkhill's lifetime was a massive two-volume tome entitled *Dictionary of the Economic Products of the Malay Peninsula,* which first appeared in 1935 but has run to several editions. Burkhill served as Director from 1912 to 1925, and Burkhill Hall, which stands on a breezy eminence in the Gardens and which used to be the Director's residence, is named after him. Built in 1867, this is one of the oldest surviving houses in Singapore — a superb example of early black and white architecture — and can nowadays be hired for private functions.

Other prominent administrators of the gardens include the botanical titan, R. E. Holttum, and his assistant, E. J. H. Corner. Like their illustrious predecessors, both were remarkable men. The published works of Holttum take up several feet of bookshelf space and include a series of dense volumes on ferns, orchids, bamboo, gingers and other Malesian monocotyledons. His best known work, however, is the popular classic *Gardening in the Lowlands of Malaya*, which first appeared in 1953. This soon became the Bible for anyone who had the slightest interest in matters horticultural and the prose reflects the gardening concerns of those far-off days: "Having decided the main division of the ground, between house, garage and (if they are to be provided) kitchen garden and nursery, ornamental garden, tennis court etc., one's next problem is the position of drives and paths." "Rather," as Bertie Wooster might have said.

E. J. H. Corner's *Wayside Trees of Malaya,* which first appeared in 1940, is another botanical classic, but he will also be long remembered for his remarkable assistants — a troop of pig-tailed macaques whom he had trained to collect flowers, fruit and leaves from the otherwise inaccessible upper reaches of tall forest trees. The cover of the first editions of *Wayside Trees* had a design, penned by Corner himself, which featured a macaque at the top of a tree with a rope hanging down, while the half-title page of the second volume bore the legend: "Malayan Trees Who Cares to Know, Upon His Shoulders Sits a Beruk" (*beruk* is the Malay term for a pig-tailed macaque).

Both Holttum and Corner were taken prisoner by the Japanese following the fall of Singapore in February 1942 — Corner was invalided out of volunteer military service after being bitten by one of his more recalcitrant plant-collecting monkeys: "That bite was my salvation," he later wrote — but managed to strike up a remarkable alliance with their captors who allowed them to continue their researches in the interests of science for the duration of the hostilities. Assisted by their Japanese colleagues, Professors Hidezo Tanakadate of Tohoku University and Kwan Koriba of the University of Kyoto, Holttum and Corner were able to preserve the Botanic Gardens more or less intact and ensure that their precious collections, both botanical and literary, were not dissipated by the winds of war. There were many, however, who viewed Holttum and Corner's efforts as nothing short of 'collaboration' with the Japanese. As Corner himself observed in his memoirs, written in retirement:

> The Japanese accused [Professor Hidezo] of being pro-British and anti-Japanese; the British internees accused me of being anti-British and pro-Japanese. We trod the centre of this precarious see-saw, and the Professor held the note from the British Governor, that no one knew of, which instructed me to hand over the records to the Japanese, not for them nor for us, but as the heirloom of the country. (*The Marquis,* 1981).

Not all the monkeys in the Gardens have been so agreeably disposed as Corner's lot (that wartime bite excepted). Up until a few years ago, the place was plagued by marauding bands of delinquent simians who were liable to hold one to ransom for a handful of peanuts. The latter could be purchased from an Indian *mamak* stall just outside the Main Gate — for a few cents, he would sell you a little cache of *kacang* wrapped up in a cone of newspaper. The monkeys, who seemed to have entered into some kind of secret pact with the peanut vendor, had their sentinels posted to keep an eye open for any likely target strolling up the main path towards the pond. At a given signal, the entire troop would descend from the trees and gather round about in a faintly menacing fashion. Their initial ploy was to fix you with a solemn and unflinching gaze, a delicately-formed hand outstretched, imploring you, with limpid eye, to toss the merest morsel of a peanut their way. If one failed to succumb to this display of monkey bathos, then more direct and unambiguous tactics were employed — the half-rising head-bob or, alternatively, a rapid raising of the eyebrows up and down, repeated several times in quick succession. In the lexicon of simian nonverbal communication, both these activities are what primatologists call 'intentional movements', the intention stated here being "If you don't hand over those peanuts pretty sharpish, boy am I gonna tear you limb from limb."

Now I don't know how many people are aware of the immense strength of a monkey, relative to a human being, but let's just say that ripping telephone directories in half would be about as easy for the average Cercopithecoid as tearing off a strip of lavatory paper for ourselves. Dismemberment, compounded by rabies, was definitely on the agenda where these fellows were concerned, and the actual attack, when it came, was always completely unpredictable and terrifying — the most belligerent male would suddenly rise off his haunches and lunge at you, yellow fangs bared in a frightful grimace, at which point the only course of action to take was to throw the peanuts in the air and leg it as fast as one could.

Having been relieved of one's nuts, so to speak, by these Cercopithecine muggers, it was safe to proceed with one's perambulations — as a small boy, I was always greatly relieved once the monkey business had been got out of the way and one could settle down to enjoy an afternoon at the Gardens.

Superficially, little seems to have changed in the Gardens since that time and all the old "favourite bits" are much as they were then. I always liked the Malayan banyan near the main entrance, rising from the ground on a tangle of prop roots, and a little further along, the swampy section, with its collection of papyrus and Siamese screw pines. Then there is the enormous Indian rubber tree at the southern end of the main lake — a truly wondrous specimen and probably the first plant I ever learnt the scientific name of — *Ficus elasticus* — which was easy to remember because it brought to mind the elasticated waist band that held up my shorts.

The lake itself was a major attraction on account of its large population of freshwater turtles, cruising in a Sargasso Sea of aquatic weeds, while the little island at the far end, crowded with soaring *nibong* palms, seemed a perfect place of enchantment — the ideal hideout for a Peter Pan and his Lost Boys. The knowledge that the lake had once harboured a man-eating crocodile helped to endorse this fantasy, though I don't suppose the historical beast had a timepiece ticking away in his belly. Nevertheless, it is true that in 1892 an itinerant crocodile decided to make himself at home in the lake and lived there peaceably until the day he ill-advisedly

71

chomped one of the gardeners, whereupon the lake was drained and the sauropod summarily dispatched.

I have actually heard that another crocodylian has recently come to reside in the murky waters of the lake. This particular specimen was previously the pet of a crazed Austrian chef, so the story goes, who used to keep him in his bathroom. One day the cook got bit and, being too big to flush down the lavatory, as I believe is customary in New York where the sewers are infested with alligators, caymens and the like, the offending reptile was surreptitiously slipped into the lake at the Gardens. No doubt this is an 'urban myth' in the making, but I'm keeping an eye open all the same.

At the northern end of the lake, the lily pond was memorable for its floating carpet of giant *Victoria amazonica*, whose leaves can grow up to six feet across. This was another "favourite bit" during my childhood, the imagined home of Beatrix Potter's Jeremy Fisher. And then, best of all, there was the jungle — the highlight of any visit to the Gardens — with its buttress-rooted forest giants and festoons of dangling lianas. Ten acres of primary jungle, with monkeys crashing through the canopy overhead, the last vestige — along with the Bukit Timah Nature Reserve — of a dipterocarp rainforest, which in Raffles' day covered almost the entire island.

I don't get wildly excited by large displays of orchids, or at least not by the sight of them arrayed, row upon serried row, as they used to be in the old Orchid Garden. I find them a bit excessive, like too many fuchsias. A single plant by itself is O.K., but *en masse* they are a trifle self-indulgent not to say slightly decadent. I am reminded here of General Sternwood's remark about orchids in *The Big Sleep*: "… nasty things. Their flesh is too much like the flesh of men. And their perfume has the rotten sweetness of a prostitute." Actually, most orchid species, or at least those that grow in the tropics, don't have a particularly noticeable fragrance, relying instead on their brilliant colours to attract pollinators. Nevertheless, one gets the General's drift.

The Victorians also had a rather ambivalent attitude towards orchids. In H. G. Wells' short story, 'The Flowering of the Strange Orchid,' published in 1895, the protagonist, Winter-Wedderburn, acquires the root of a unknown species whose discoverer had perished in mysterious circumstances — his bloodless corpse was found, half submerged, in a mangrove swamp with one of these strange plants crushed beneath it. Winter-Wedderburn should have known better, but despite the reservations of his housekeeper, he goes ahead and plants the thing in his conservatory where it grows vigorously, turning into a huge triffid-like affair with an intricate web of sinister aerial roots that look like groping fingers. Then flower buds appear and when they open they release a sickly-sweet perfume which overwhelms Winter-Wedderburn, rendering him senseless. The deadly roots envelop him like haustoria, draining his lifeblood from him and Winter-Wedderburn is only saved, just in the nick of time, by his quick-witted housekeeper who hurls a brick through the glass of the conservatory, allowing an icy, winter's wind to enter which disperses the narcotic fragrance and withers the monstrous vegetable.

A visit to Singapore's Botanic Gardens today is not really as hazardous as might be imagined from this narrative. It is highly unlikely that one would encounter a tiger there, while even the monkeys are long gone, though there may be a crocodile in the pond and it might be as well to stand back from the orchids. No, it is a sublime experience, especially at dusk when the first bats take to the wing and the feathery *nibong* palms are etched against a darkening sky. I have been there on several such evenings in the past few months to listen to a programme of music in the excellent 'Jazz in the Park' series — our modern counterpart of the brass bands of my grandmother's day. On the last occasion, it was the eve of the Autumnal Chong Quai celebrations, otherwise known as the 'Mooncake Festival', and many people had brought traditional, candle-lit paper lanterns with them. Little pools of coloured light dipped and floated across the Palm Valley, as a luminescent moon rose above the dark trees of the jungle opposite and the first stars appeared in an indigo sky over ahead. Music may well be "the food of love," but as the Bard's contemporary, Francis Bacon, observed: "God Almighty first planted a garden. And indeed it is the purest of human pleasures" (*Essays*: 'Of Gardens').

WHERE PARROT ISLANDS ANCHORED LIE

I should like to rise and go,
Where the golden apples grow;
Where below another sky
Parrot islands anchored lie,
And, watched by cockatoos and goats,
Lonely Crusoes building boats …

— Robert Louis Stevenson, *A Child's Garden of Verses* (1885) —

An Italian friend who came to visit me, here in Singapore, a couple of years ago, was very insistent about wanting to see the sea. I was fairly noncommittal, but she kept on expressing her desire to "*vedere il mare,*" so in the end I told her to take a 167 bus down to the Raffles Hotel and then to keep on walking in a straight line for about a kilometre and a half until she came to the sea. My friend returned at the end of the day, hot, tired and a looking a trifle disappointed. "*O capito,*" was all she said, "I have understood." But I didn't understand, and it took me some time until I realised what all the fuss was about. Singapore is a tropical island and for Enrica, as is true for many other people, especially those who live in colder climes, tropical islands are meant to be a kind of earthly paradise — they are places of natural beauty, bounty and bliss, the domain of Daphnis and Chloë, where sensuous, clean-limbed, brown-skinned natives recline beneath swaying palm trees disporting themselves to the ethereal music of aeolian harps. No doubt most people recognise this vision as a somewhat exaggerated fantasy, an impossible confection of scenes from *Blue Hawaii* and the stories of James Mitchener, augmented by half-remembered passages from books that children used to read, but probably don't any longer — *Treasure Island, The Coral Island, Robinson Crusoe, Swiss Family Robinson* and the rest. Nevertheless, the idea still has a powerful currency in the collective imagination of the West, a vision of a latter-day Garden of Eden supplemented by a cornucopia of Bounty bars and Malibu fruit juice. Modern Singapore, however, is a far cry from Captain Cook's Tahiti or Gauguin's mythologising in the Marquesas and I could understand my Italian friend's disappointment.

Certainly, the artificial beaches of the East Coast Park, with their carefully laid out bicycle paths and strategically placed barbecue pits hold little attraction for me, while the less-than-limpid waters that listlessly lap the shoreline look far from inviting. But it wasn't always so. There was a time, not so many years ago, when the seas around Singapore were as clear as glass and one could spot a sea urchin with its pearly 'eye' on a sandy bottom from a boat in fifteen feet of water.

In those days we used to visit Pulau Damar, a little island that lay just off the West Coast, but which has long since been swallowed up by the Jurong land reclamation scheme that turned a little archipelago of rocky islets, with coconut palms and white sandy beaches, into an industrial park. Back then, in the shallow waters that surrounded Pulau Damar there were coral reefs which one could wade out to at low tide and standing thigh-deep in water observe all manner of interesting marine life at one's feet — little shoals of brilliant-blue damsel fish or brown and white 'clowns' threading their way in and out of sea anemones whose tentacles wafted gently back and forth in the motion of the shallow waves. Fat sea cucumbers littered the bottom like large turds and sometimes a blue-spotted ray in its distinctive polka dot attire would suddenly rise up in a cloud of sand, to flit across the shallows like the shadow of a bird in flight. If one was very lucky, one might even catch a glimpse of a spectacularly-hued nudibranch, the Carmen Miranda of marine molluscs, undulating between the coral heads like a runaway blancmange.

Back then, going to Pulau Damar was like spending a weekend in the country — one stayed the night. There was a bungalow for rental on the island, or maybe it belonged to friends — as a child one is blissfully removed from the need to organise things, they just happen, like sequences in a film. A boat appears at a jetty and the next moment the party and all its provisions are on board and we are chugging along a palm-fringed coastline where little inlets lead to Malay *kampong*s, half-hidden amongst the trees. The boat smells of diesel oil and fish and its wooden decks are bleached white by the sun. We pass a *sampan* with a much-weathered fisherman squatting implacably in the stern-sheets beneath a huge conical sun hat. He returns our wave, and we leave him bobbing in our wake. Then a house with a long, low verandah, standing in a grove of coconut palms, comes into view. "We're here!" someone cries, and in a moment the bows of boat are run up on to the white sand and we are wading ashore, an overnight case clutched tightly to our chest — "Don't let it get wet, it's only made of cardboard!"

The sea is warm, the sand is hot and the stretch of coarse grass leading up the bungalow, prickly beneath one's bare feet. It is the middle of the day and the sun is ferocious, its glare intense. A chorus of cicadas comes from the coconut grove behind the house, like the whine of a timber saw, and the still air hangs heavily about our ears.

Later, as the afternoon wears on and a sea breeze disperses the heat of the middle hours of the day, rich colours flood back into the landscape. Huge vanilla cumulus clouds, a thousand feet high, billow on the horizon where the deep water has turned a cobalt blue. There are sails out there — a Malay fishing fleet from one of the villages along the coast — but closer at hand, the tide is out and it is time to explore the coral gardens that lie just a few yards from the shore.

Later still, the sun has set and the first stars have appeared overhead, complementing the cluster of twinkling lights which glister on an unseen horizon — the boats of nocturnal fishermen bobbing on an ocean, black as ink. The aroma of grilled *ikan kurau* and freshly-cut limes competes with scent of frangipani in the garden and the salty dampness of seaweed on the beach. The bright lights of the house stream across the lawn and some one is summoning me to go to bed, but I don't mind — the sun and sea air have spun their soporific spell and I am happy to retire with the dulcet sound of waves upon the shore in my ears and the comforting murmur of grown-up voices on the verandah. I hear the clink of ice in a whiskey glass, punctuated by the fizzing of a soda siphon, while somewhere at the back of the house, a nightjar begins his nightly 'tock, tock, tock.'

If one didn't go to Pulau Damar, then at the other end of Singapore Island, there was always the excellent Casuarina Hotel, whose rubble today lies impacted beneath the concrete runways of Changi Airport. The

Casuarina Hotel had a spacious terrace which ended in a sea wall and steps that led down to the beach. Sun umbrellas provided shade during the day while at night the grown-ups danced to the gentle rhythms of a Philippino guitar trio plucking away at Nat 'King' Cole numbers, beneath a silvery moon.

At one end of the beach there was a rocky promontory with huge boulders to clamber over and rock pools left by the retreating tide. This was a magical world of starfish and Crustacea, limpets and periwinkles — an aquatic microcosm where translucent shrimps, with tiny, black, pinprick eyes, hovered in the shade of overhanging rocks and there was a crab in every crevice, though one had to endure several minutes of perfect stillness, before they would reveal themselves.

Changi, with its fine white-sand beaches had always been a popular place for swimming since the earliest days of Singapore and in the 1840s a government lodge or "sanitaria" was erected there. One or two people built private seaside bungalows in the vicinity of Fairy Point in the nineteenth century and sago plantations flourished for a while in the 1860s, but up until the late 1930s, Changi remained, the beach aside, a place of mangrove swamp and virgin forest. In 1938, however, with the prospect of an Asian war menacing on the horizon, work began on what became known as 'Fortress Changi', a formidable battery of heavy artillery and anti-aircraft guns to defend the eastern sea approaches to the new naval base in the Johor Straits. The latter was described by the *Sydney Morning Herald* as "The Gibraltar of the East, ... the bastion of British Might."

Fortress Changi was completed in 1941 to the accompaniment of further superlatives: "a newer, bigger and better Gibraltar, one of the most formidable concatenations of naval military and strategic power ever put together anywhere." The rest, as they say, is history.

Nothing much remains, as far as I am aware, of Fortress Changi today, but I remember that there was still a concrete gun emplacement on the beach in the early 1960s, standing grey and sinister, just above the high-water mark, its weathered surfaces crumbling in the sea air, its bevelled-edged gun ports like sightless eyes, an ironic reminder of British coastal defences against a seaborne invasion that never came.

The drive to Changi was part of the fun of going there. The most direct route was to take the Changi Road, but it was more agreeable to go via the East Coast Road, which in those days did indeed run along the eastern shoreline of Singapore. After leaving Katong and the fishing village of Bedok — a good place for seafood — the road would pass through groves of coconut palms, past crumbling seaside villas with overgrown gardens and collapsing sea walls. There always seemed to be a stiff onshore breeze blowing through the crowns of the coconut trees, bending their slender trunks and rattling their fronds. And with the wind came the salty tang of the sea mixed with the smell of dried fish, seaweed and, at low tide, mud. "A good day for sailing," my father would remark, a part of him secretly wishing he had accepted that offer to crew on a racing dragon at the Royal Singapore Yacht Club.

Every so often, one would pass a Malay *kampong* with neat little *atap*-thatched houses standing on stilts amongst the coconut palms. Chickens scrabbled in the freshly swept earth, while brightly coloured *sarong*s and fishing nets hung between the trees to dry. *Ikan bilis* and shrimps lay on mats in the sun by their millions, watched over by small children with long poles to shoo away itinerant birds and beasts, while further back from the road, where the soil was less sandy, there were little plantations of cassava and banana trees. And every mile or so one would come across a wooden Chinese shophouse by the side of the road, its display of merchandise a brilliant splash of colour, with a few chairs and tables under the trees which allowed the proprietor to augment his retail business by doubling as a *kopi tiam*.

Seen from a passing car window the scene seemed timeless and idyllic, but we know better now — life was hard for these people of the Singapore littoral with few material rewards, poor sanitation and a general absence

of public utilities. Today, every one of these fishing villages has disappeared, their inhabitants long ago dispersed to the HDB estates of modern Singapore. At the same time, reclaimed land projects have dramatically redefined the contours of our island home so that the East Coast Road now finds itself at some remove from the sea. You can, however, get a good idea of what it used to be like from those old Malay movies featuring P. Ramlee which are shown on television from time to time — quite a lot of *Penarik Beca* takes place on the East Coast, as well as downtown Singapore, if any one is interested in renting the video.

Loyang was a good place to go if one wanted to get away from other people — the coastline there was covered in a kind of scrubby vegetation — a tangle of sea almonds, screw pines and sea lettuce — but there were tracks leading down to the shore which you could just about get a car down. My father had a Citroen DS in those days — the only one in Singapore — which had the famous adjustable pneumatic suspension system that could be raised or lowered according to the nature of the terrain. We would pause at the beginning of a track leading down to a secluded cove to pump up the suspension to maximum clearance and then proceed along the trail, pushing aside the coarse *lalang* grass and wild lantana bushes with the spatulate bonnet, confident in the knowledge that even the deepest pothole could be safely traversed by this triumph of French engineering.

On arrival at the beach, a tarpaulin would be rigged up between the trees for shade and driftwood collected for a fire before a tour of inspection of the little bay was mounted to see what interesting things had been washed up since the last visit. Inevitably, there were several dozen rubber flip-flops (though they never made a pair), but curiously there were also an extraordinary number of plastic dolls, or rather parts of plastic dolls — heads, arms, legs and the occasionally limbless torso — washed up on the shoreline like the remnants of a cannibal feast.

My father's preferred mode of relaxation was to float on a Lilo a little way off the beach, enjoying the gentle motion of the waves, while refreshing himself from a chilled bottle of Tiger which I would periodically be called upon to replenish from the shore. Unfortunately, this pastime caused considerable anxiety to the family dog, a corpulent but amiable creature who went by the name of Hamish. The latter would stand barking in the shallows or else swim out to my father and circle anxiously around him until we feared that he would drown through exhaustion.

Eventually a solution was found when my father taught the dog to float along side him on a second Lilo, whereupon the two of them then spent many happy hours together bobbing about on the waves some twenty to thirty yards from the shore. It must be said, however, that Hamish never entirely lost the slightly worried frown that wrinkled his brow until their return to dry land — no sea dog he!

Sometimes, when energy was lacking for the preparation of a full-scale picnic, we would repair instead to the old Sea View Hotel at Katong. The latter was a splendid remnant of the colonial era with a long history dating back to 1906 when it had first opened with forty rooms, a beer garden, tennis courts and a swimming enclosure. At one time the hotel belonged to the influential Jewish businessman Sir Manassesh Meyer, but in 1923 the Sarkies brothers of Raffles Hotel fame took on the lease and embarked upon a series of improvements. The prevailing architectural style of these new additions was tropical Deco — a little bit of old Miami Beach amongst the coconut groves of Katong — and they included a light and airy ballroom which was open on one side to the sea.

In my childhood, Sunday's curry tiffin was served on a long verandah that was built right up to the very edge of the water and I can well remember the waves dashing upon the seawall at our feet. As in all my recollections of the East Coast, there is a strong breeze blowing, soughing through the coconut palms that surrounded the Sea View and lifting the corners of the linen table cloths.

At that time the Sea View was a bit of a swinging hot spot with an Italian dance band cutting the ice at the Chicken Inn — a popular nightclub within the hotel. But that kind of lifestyle, when men still wore sharkskin dinner jackets in the unairconditioned tropical heat, was rapidly coming to an end and as Ray Tyers poignantly puts it in his book, *Singapore Then and Now* (1975), when the band left "… silence and the elements took over."

I don't know when the hotel closed or whether any of the buildings are still standing — it's many years since I was last there and the sea has long since retreated before the bulldozers and earthmovers of Singapore's land reclamation engineers. Nor have I been back in a long while to the Singapore Swimming Club, which used to be just down the road from the Sea View. The Singapore Swimming Club was also beside the sea at one time, but now has been left high and dry by the amoeba-like advance of Singapore's shore line. Its origins date back to 1839 when an *atap*-roofed bungalow was rented by a coterie of beach enthusiasts at Sandy Point, at the very tip of Tanjong Rhu. Later a more substantial club house was built with a concrete pier and diving platform and this became the regular meeting place for those who liked to spend their weekends by the sea.

In the early days and up until the advent of refrigeration in the late 1930s, the coastal waters around Singapore were the happy hunting ground of rapacious sharks who regularly claimed the lives of those who ill-advisedly decided to take a dip. Given the hazardous nature of the seas, would-be bathers took the precaution of swimming in special enclosures, or *pagar*s as they were called, *pagar* being the Malay word for a fence. Sandy Point, however, was deemed to be safe on account of a long shallow bar running parallel to the beach, over which, it was assumed, sharks would not presume to venture. But venture they did, or at least one particular specimen who took a club member in 1926, after which a *pagar* was built.

Not that this was fail-safe, as John Forrester recalls when, as a small boy, the ship on which he was travelling from China back to England put into Singapore and he was taken for a day out at the Swimming Club:

> It was in the sea and had nets all around it, but a shark got in and took one of the lady swimmers. This very brave man was on the raft that she had just dived off and he dived on top of the shark and got her back on to the raft, minus a leg. We were on the beach at the time and there was a terrible commotion. I remember being taken very quickly back to the ship (cited in Charles Allen's *Tales from the South China Seas*, 1983).

Land was acquired for a freshwater pool in 1927 and the latter was officially opened by Governor Sir Cecil Clementi Smith, in December 1931. I nearly drowned in it once, but was saved by my mother who dived in fully-clothed to rescue me. I must have been very young, for I have been a pretty good swimmer for as long as I can remember. Nevertheless, I can still distinctly recollect the curious sensation of being at the bottom of the pool and the strange distortion of sound that occurs in such circumstances.

Today, as one speeds along East Coast Parkway, one can still catch a glimpse of the magnificent club house, designed by local Modernist, Frank

Brewer, in 1935 — I particularly like the beautiful sculptural forms of the high-diving boards. But the place is landlocked now and the sandy beach on which the club was built, and where one could pick up dazzling plates of mother-of-pearl, has been interred beneath an expressway.

This is pretty much what has happened to most of Singapore's original coastline over the past one hundred and fifty years, ever since the British first began to fill in Telok Ayer Bay back in the 1860s. Today, Changi has become a synonym for what is arguably the world's finest airport, while most of the East Coast has been carefully recreated as a public pleasure park. A slip road takes you from the ECP to a carpark located within easy walking distance of a seafood hawker centre, with a MacDonald's nearby for emergencies. There are changing room facilities and exercise areas, and a few shops for recreational purposes. Air-conditioning is available for those who feel like a fish out of water without it, but for the more seriously outdoor types, there is, of course, the beach — teams of experts have advised on the landscaping and the sand has been especially imported from Indonesia, with very precise instructions regarding the size of the grains. Though roller-blading is the number-one sport, you can hire a bicycle, a pedalo or a kayak. And you are never out of sight of a litter bin. But is this all it takes to create a paradise? Can the simulacrum be better than the original, the artificial more pleasing than the real?

For my own part, I know that a tropical island paradise, untouched by the hand of man, does exist because I have been there — a remote island in the Nicobar group, with jungle-clad hills and a palm-fringed shore. Here we dropped anchor in a cerulean bay beneath an azure sky; three fathoms deep and one could see the shadow of our boat on the sandy bottom. No "lonely Crusoes building boats," no footprints to disturb the soft white sand, not even a rubber flip-flop revealed the trace of man. But there were plenty of brightly coloured parakeets screeching in the tree tops and the sea was literally teaming with fish — one could see lunch arriving from afar and rising to the bait in those pellucid seas.

Our stay was brief — just long enough to roast a grouper on the beach — but the memory of that unsullied earthly paradise remains. And this may be the more important thing, for as Vita Sackville-West once observed, "to hope for Paradise is to live in Paradise, a very different thing from actually getting there" (*Passenger to Tehran,* 1926).

UTILITAS, FIRMITAS ET VENUSTAS

In Architecture as in all other Operative Arts, the end must direct the Operation. The end is to build well. Well building hath three conditions. Commoditie, Firmenes, and Delight.

— Sir Henry Wotton, *The Elements of Architecture* (1624) —

❖

The black and white colonial bungalow in Singapore is one of the most perfect of architectural creations, combining the elegance of Classical forms with a Jacobean rustic charm, and yet at the same time providing a sensible and ecologically sound response to the demands of designing for a tropical environment.

When I was a child, my best friend, Simon, used to live in one of these beautiful houses — I think it was number one Seton Close, which stood, together with half a dozen similar houses, in a shady bower, just off Tanglin Road. Amazingly they are still there today, though I believe that number one was pulled down some years ago. I remember the long shadows of late afternoon and the play of sunlight on the stuccoed columns; huge trees and neatly mown lawns; a grass tennis court. This is where I learnt to ride a bicycle and where I first ate prawns — I didn't realise, on the initial encounter with said Crustacea, that one should generally remove the head, legs and carapace before putting them in one's mouth and I can remember stoically crunching my way through a *mee goreng* lunch wondering just what it was that made people add these horrid little creatures to a perfectly good plate of noodles.

And then there was an enormous Indian bean tree whose hard and shiny, blood-red seeds, the size of milk teeth, lay scattered round about in great profusion. We gathered jars of them — it seemed impossible to us that something so beautiful could have no intrinsic commercial value. And indeed, in those days one could buy the same seeds down in Little India, which had had their innards scooped out and tiny ivory elephants no bigger than a mosquito placed inside. I haven't seen one of these exquisitely-worked little microscopic sculptures in years — I wonder if they still make them. I suppose not, what with the ban on ivory trade and all that, which of course is a good and proper thing, but they were rather marvellous, those minuscule white pachyderms hiding like little elephant homunculi inside their suit of vermilion armour.

But anyway, we were talking about bungalows. The term 'bungalow', today, has come to have rather ambivalent connotations in the English language. Here in Singapore, where the long shadows of late Empire still linger in the leafy enclaves of Goodwood Hill, Nassim Road, Alexandra Park and other salubrious residential backwaters which have yet to be supplanted by condominiums and HDB estates, the term bungalow can still be used without occasioning a snigger. Back in England, however, the word has acquired quite different significations, being irredeemably linked to images of suburban conformity and homogeneity, cul-de-sacs and privet hedges, a dreary social and physical environment which is portrayed in pathological terms as "bungalow blight." And rightly so — the latter condition is especially prevalent along England's southern coastline, where in the past seventy years an ugly rash of horrible little single-storeyed dwellings has spread like athlete's foot to just about every cove and bay between Margate and Bognor Regis.

To the extent that the term bungalow is used in this context to refer to a vernacular architectural tradition consisting of simple, low-cost, low-rise housing, affordable by the masses, the etymology of the word has come full circle. The term is derived from the Hindi word, '*bangala*', meaning 'of' or 'from Bengal' and originally referred specifically to European houses in India. These were generally a single-storey dwelling with a verandah on all sides and a pitched roof with overhanging eaves to keep off the sun's rays and the monsoon rains. The basic form was adapted, as the name suggests, from native vernacular traditions in Bengal of which there were two basic types. The first of these was a fairly humble single-storeyed hut with a distinctive crescent-shaped roof made of thatch which drooped down over the external walls and was supported by free standing wooden posts to create a shaded verandah.

Alternatively, the term *bangala* could also be applied to a building with a pitched roof of tile or thatch which had a second roof at a lower level that projected outwards, again creating a shady verandah which protected the core of the building from the sun and rain.

Quite which of these two forms provided the original inspiration for an Englishman's house in India is uncertain, but once adopted, it became the archetype for a domestic colonial architecture which spread, not only throughout the whole of India, but also to every distant outpost of the British Empire, from Wagga Wagga to the shores of Queen Charlotte Sound.

And that was just the beginning. In the middle to late nineteenth century the bungalow was successively embraced by both the Picturesque and the Arts-and-Craft Movements, which imbued its exotic otherness with a Romantic rusticism that was subsequently conflated with a no-nonsense, back-to-basics approach to architecture as advocated by William Morris and his merry band of Morris-men. Not that there was anything particularly sensible about building bungalows in England, whose wet and wintry climate was not especially well-suited to an architectural style which made a virtue of wide and airy verandahs.

The bungalow also caught on on the other side of the Atlantic where, once it had been adapted to local conditions, both climatic and cultural, it evolved into a fine and distinctive architectural tradition of its own.

Perhaps the most curious usage of the word I have come across is in the detective who-done-it, *Behind that Curtain*, by Earl Derr Biggers, featuring the inscrutable Sergeant Charlie Chan, star sleuth of the Honolulu Police Force. One of the central characters in the novel is the young, San Francisco millionaire playboy, Barry Kirk, who has a bachelor penthouse pad on the twentieth floor of the building that bears his family name. Mr. Biggers tells us that "The Kirk Building was architecturally perfect, in the excellent taste that marked the family ever since the first Dawson Kirk had made his millions and gone his way. Now it was the particular hobby of young Barry Kirk who lived in bachelor splendor in the spacious but breezy bungalow on its roof". Some hobby! Some bungalow! The word has certainly travelled a long way from the humble, single-storeyed, grass-thatched bower that it originally denoted in Bengal.

But to get back to the black and white colonial bungalow here in Singapore, strictly speaking the term bungalow refers to a single-storey building — this was the original form that the bungalow took and is the general accepted meaning of the word both in Europe and the Americas. However, as John Cameron observed in his account of *Our Tropical Possessions in India Malay*, published in 1865, the term is "often applied to any style of dwelling-house in the East" and it is in this capacity that I use it now.

The earliest colonial bungalows in the Straits Settlements — the East India Company stations of Penang, Malacca and Singapore — were essentially Indian imports. By this time, however, the original form had undergone substantial modifications and at the upper end of the scale was far removed from its modest agrarian origins. European influences, and in particular the Classically-inspired, Palladian architecture of the Regency period in England, had imposed a symmetrical plan and the introduction of an upper storey, or *piano nobile*, as the main living floor. In this last respect there was an obvious parallel with the native Malay house which was also raised off the ground on posts in order to increase ventilation and reduced humidity. Other correspondences included full-length louvred shutters to maximise the through-flow of air and pitched roofs with widely overhanging eaves which not only provided shade, but also cut down glare. Furthermore, the verandah was a key element in both architectural traditions, providing a light and breezy space for daily activities and social intercourse.

In the case of colonial architecture, the essentially rustic nature of the bungalow was ennobled by the use of Classical elements — Doric or Tuscan orders of columns and the like — but an overall correspondence between the two types of architecture is unmistakable. No doubt this was partly due to a kind of parallel evolution — a resort to similar solutions when addressing the problems of designing for a hot and humid monsoon climate — but there also seems to have been a considerable cross-fertilisation of ideas between Malay and colonial architectures in the nineteenth century, making it difficult sometimes, to unravel which tradition provided the original source of inspiration for many shared architectural features.

The so-called 'black and white' bungalow of the 1920s and '30s represents the apogee of an architectural tradition and a high-water mark in tropical design, where sensible architectural solutions to the vicissitudes of the equatorial climate were equalled by an elegance of form and harmonious proportions. I have based the following description on my memories of the house at Seton Close, which in my mind represents the quintessential black and white bungalow.

The ground floor was typically constructed from brick and featured a covered porch, or *porte cochère*, framed by paired Tuscan or Roman Doric columns which supported a projecting verandah above. The upper storey was of wood — a half-timbered affair, with plaited bamboo panels plastered over with lime. The main structural elements of this upper storey were invariably painted black while the panels in between were painted white.

In this last respect their appearance bore a superficial resemblance to the traditional timber-framed vernacular architecture of England which had recently enjoyed something of a stylistic revival, courtesy of the Arts-and-Crafts Movement. It was this characteristic 'colour-scheme' which naturally gave rise to the descriptive label 'black and white' as a generic term for this type of architecture, though the incorporation of Classical elements was more Jacobean than late-Medieval .

The ground floor usually comprised a spacious reception room and dining area (the kitchen and servants' quarters being removed some distance at the back of the house), but the main living space was on the floor above. Here, the rooms were symmetrically arranged, with bedrooms and bathrooms placed on either side of a central salon. The latter extended over the *porte cochère* and was the principal area for socialising and relaxation. Open on three sides, it represented the ultimate expression of a verandah lifestyle which had evolved in colonial India during the eighteenth century. A cantilevered balcony running round the outside of the upper storey connected the bedrooms and bathrooms and provided alternative spaces for daily activities while allowing for the discrete passage of servants.

The last of the black and whites were built in the years leading up to the Second World War. After the cessation of hostilities and the restoration of a British colonial government, new sensibilities prevailed, which is where my father, Percy Robert Davison, enters the story.

Born in Singapore between the wars, my father, like so many sons of the Empire, was sent away to boarding school in England at a very early age in order to be thoroughly inculcated into the ways of an Englishman. He was brought back to Singapore, for a year, when he was eleven, in order to be re-acquainted with his father whom he had not seen since the age of eight. During this period he was taught by a private tutor. Then, when the year was up, he was packed off to England again, to continue his education there, and this is how he came to enrol at the Architectural Association in Bedford Square, London, shortly before the outbreak of the Second World War. As it happens, my father actually wanted to be an artist, but my paternal grandfather found the idea preposterous, so he elected to become an architect instead.

When war was declared, my father volunteered for the Navy and it was not until the conclusion of hostilities that he was able to resume his studies at the Architectural Association, or the AA as it is more familiarly known. At some point he was a town planner in Margate, but memories of an Eastern childhood preyed upon his mind and not long after graduating he was happy to return to Singapore as a municipal architect with the Singapore Improvement Trust, the colonial forerunner of the

Housing Development Board. This was in the early fifties. A brief spell back in England convinced him that those cold and misty shores were definitely not for him and he returned to Singapore once more, this time as one of the founding partners in the Singapore office of Raglan Squire & Partners (today's RSP).

Modernism was the thing in those days and that meant flat roofs, plain facades, buildings raised off the ground on columns and a much professed abhorrence for even the slightest hint of ornamentation — every architectural feature or component should be there solely to serve the purpose it was designed for; decoration just wasn't on the agenda. And rather like Henry Ford's pronouncement on the Model T, you could have any colour you liked so long as it was white.

Mies van der Rohe, Walter Gropius, Le Corbusier and of course that old maverick from another time and place, Frank Lloyd Wright, were the high priests of this 'cult of the new' and they could do no wrong. My father used to tell the story of how he once attended a lecture by 'Corbu' at the AA, during which le Maître had illustrated his thesis with lightning sketches on huge sheets of paper which he tore from a large roll of paper. At the end of the lecture, my father said, pandemonium broke out as the students, of one accord, stampeded across the lecture hall and fell upon the waste paper basket in an unseemly scrabble to retrieve one of these discarded 'masterpieces.'

Some years later and many thousands of miles away from Bedford Square (the home of the AA), my father tried his hand at emulating the master himself and built a perfect gem of a Modernist villa for a very progressive Chinese client in Newton Road, just a stone's throw from the Circus. My father's house was pure Corbusian in conception, with a little touch of Frank Lloyd Wright at the bottom where a short flight of stairs led up from the driveway to a raised terrace whose vertical surfaces were faced with rough-cut stones.

This was in 1959 and the Modernist Movement in Europe was already half a century old by this time, but here in Singapore the building must

have come as quite an eye-opener to those unaccustomed to the new aesthetics which favoured plain surfaces, sharp edges and strong horizontals. The trouble with flat roofs, and all the other bits and pieces that one associates with the Modern Movement, is that they don't really work in a tropical environment. In fact flat roofs don't really work in any kind of environment, except perhaps the Sahara where there is almost no precipitation of any kind, save for the occasional drop of guano from a migrant bird passing on high. But flat roofs and all the rest were definitely Modern, there could be no denying that, and that's what really mattered then. And I suspect, that in my father's case at least, there may have been an element of *épater le Bourgeoisie* involved — after all, here was a man who wore suede boots and sported a bow tie (in later life it was replaced by a boot lace, in the manner of Doc Holiday), and who also let his hair curl over the back of his shirt collar, all of which was considered rather unconventional if not downright Bohemian by the standards of the day.

But if Le Corbusier's houses may not always have worked very well — the Villa Savoy, which is often held up to be his masterpiece, was more successfully employed as a hay barn than as a "machine for living in" — at least his architecture had a clear cut, if rather austere, aesthetic sensibility which delighted in the assembly of pure geometrical forms and the subtle play of light and shadow. Unfortunately, in the case of the modern Singaporean residential architecture, such sensitivities have been bulldozed into the ground and aesthetics have been thrown out the window, along with any notion of relating the house to the physical, historical or cultural environment in which it is located.

Looking back on the building boom which has so dramatically altered the suburban landscape of our island home in the past ten to fifteen years, one feels that what we have experienced here is a new kind of architectural blight — a tropical variety which can be found throughout Southeast Asia from Hanoi to Surabaya, but which is especially virulent in Singapore. The single defining feature of this new plague upon our houses, which is threatening to reach epidemic proportions, is monstrousness. My *Websters' Unabridged* defines the term 'monstrous' as meaning, among other things, "frightful or hideous, esp. of appearance; extremely ugly ... extraordinarily great; huge; immense," which is precisely what is wrong, to my mind, with this emergent architectural tradition. Put simply, the modern suburban villa in Southeast Asia is a monstrosity.

To begin with, the scale is all wrong. The typical contemporary house, here in Singapore, would appear to have been designed for a race of giants, a family of supermen some one and a half times taller and broader than the average human being; everything seems to be too big and out of proportion. Commensurate with this is the amount of land required to build a single dwelling nowadays: big houses take up more space and today's homes are usually built to within half a centimetre of the boundary, leaving scarcely room for a blade of grass, let alone anything one might properly call a garden. And then of course there is the matter of style. The formula here seems to be 'Anything goes and the more of it the better,' but the end result, more often than not, tends to be a ghastly pastiche of half a dozen different architectural traditions, cobbled together in a bizarre assembly of Corinthian columns, mansard roofs, Baroque scrolls, cantilevered balconies, picture windows and Art Deco doo-dahs. Moreover, every window has been hermetically sealed with blue-tinted glass and once inside one has more chance of catching a severe chill than inhaling a breath of fresh air.

The great Victorian architects of the last part of the nineteenth century were able to successfully combine a number of different building traditions and architectural histories to create a dynamic, sometimes whimsical, at times even downright fantastical, style of architecture which we know today as the Eclectic School. A handful of more recent exponents have achieved similar, if more modest, successes, though the underlying ethos nowadays is more ironic than celebratory. Here in Singapore, however, the post-Modernist experiment, one feels, has gone off the rails and the results have been worse than a dog's breakfast — eclecticism this certainly ain't.

In this nightmare world of architectural guacamole, the Classical pediment or Venetian baluster has become a mere cypher, often with no logical relation to the design of the building, either in structural terms or even simply as a decorative device. But where there are signs there are meanings, and the intention here, one assumes, is to convey the understanding that those who inhabit these superannuated wedding cakes are not only the heirs to an immense fortune, but are also persons of great sophistication and refinement. The first of these conditions is easily met for as Le Corbusier himself remarked: "If you want to see bad taste, go into the houses of the rich." As for sophistication and refinement, I rest my case.

And so, by way of conclusion, let us return to the black and white bungalow for a final look. As we stand on the threshold of the twenty-first century and are assailed by apocalyptic visions of global warming, environmental degradation and a drastic curtailment of life on earth as we have known it (all of which I take perfectly seriously), it is not the present generation of houses which appear to me to be modern, in terms of their design principles and use of materials. Rather it is the bungalows of the pre-war era which seem to be more in accord with the call for an environmentally-sensitive architecture, an architecture which seeks to conserve energy rather than carelessly consume profligate amounts of the stuff in order to compensate for the consequences of poor and ill-considered building formulas.

The black and white bungalow needed no air-conditioning units, running night and day to be habitable. Nor did they require thousands of cubic metres of ferroconcrete and a million dollars spent on marble and other exotic materials to achieve a classical elegance. Instead they made do with humble bricks and mortar, plus a few locally-available timbers which would still be cheap if the region's forests hadn't been cut down for concrete shuttering and disposable chopsticks. Lastly, but not least, the black and white bungalow was a comfortable home to live in, commodious yet restrained, while remaining pleasing to the eye.

Two thousand years ago, the Roman architect Vitruvius sat down to write his famous treatise *On Architecture*, in which he set out his views on what conditions needed to be fulfilled in order to create the perfect building. There were three, he decided, all of which must be present in order to achieve this distinction. They were: *utilitas, firmitas* and *venustas* — utility, firmness (or strength), and beauty. The black and white bungalow perfectly realised all three of these virtues, I believe, but I don't suppose we shall see their like again on this sunny isle. It would be a shame to pull down any more of them.

RIDING THE MAGIC ARROW

For my part, I travel not to go anywhere, but to go.
I travel for travel's sake. The great affair is to move.
— Robert Louis Stevenson, *Travels with a Donkey* (1879) —

It is still agreeable to travel by train in the Malay Peninsula, but it is not so much of an adventure as it once was. Nowadays, the seats are comfortably upholstered, the carriages air-conditioned, there are video entertainments and the coffee is served in Styrofoam cups with a plastic swizzle stick instead of a teaspoon. All of these, are no doubt regarded by many as substantial improvements over the bad old days when one proceeded in cattle trucks, but to my mind they bring little genuine pleasure. What's more, you don't seem to be able to buy a bottle of Tiger Beer on board train any more.

In those 'bad old days' — and I am speaking here of no more than ten to twenty years ago — air-conditioning meant having all the windows open and 'comfortable' was a relative term, but to take the train from, say, Singapore to Kuala Lumpur, or better still, from Gemas to Kota Bahru, was to embark upon a journey of Adventure and Romance. Some sense of this can still be picked up at the railway station down in Tanjong Pagar. This Art Deco masterpiece, standing beside the elevated section of Ayer Rajah Expressway, represents the southern-most extremity of a railway network which, were it not for wars, border restrictions and general neglect, would allow one to travel by train all the way from Singapore to Phnom Penh, calling at all stations in between.

The entrance façade is dominated by four huge figures representing Agriculture, Commerce, Transport and Industry. Like latter-day saints, their separate identities are signalled by attributes associated with their calling: Agriculture grasps a sickle, while Commerce dangles a bag of filthy lucre; Transport is bowed under the weight of an immense beam and Industry brandishes a massive sledge hammer. Over each of their heads, there is a shield emblazoned with a single capital letter — 'F', 'M', 'S' and 'R' — which are of course the initials of the Federated Malay States Railways. The little rush of nostalgia for the not so distant, still-remembered past that this recognition brings, is a rare sensation in modern Singapore, where anything old which has not been already demolished has been subjected to such a radical face-lift that any sense of history or the passage of time has been just about completely erased along with the patina of age.

A large sign bearing the legend "Welcome to Malaysia," greets one in the shadows of the *porte-cochère*, and indeed one only has to place a foot inside the railway station to feel that one is already abroad. The atmosphere changes perceptibly: Malay is the common language spoken here and one senses a distinct loosening of belt and tie, a slackening of pace, a feeling of having arrived somewhere else, though one has yet to even board a train.

The high-ceilinged departures and arrivals hall is dominated by six huge murals depicting various scenes of Malayan life in pre-war days. Hand-painted ceramic tiles conjure up a pastoral idyll of rubber plantations, rice fields and coconut trees. A bullock cart slowly lumbers by an itinerant pineapple seller sitting by the roadside and even the opencast tin mine manages to look suitably rustic. My favourite panel, though, is the one representing maritime trade, the lifeblood of the colony. This features a square-rigged barque from times gone by, a Malay *kolek* and a Chinese junk, and a steam ship with red and black funnels like those of the Queen Mary. I think I like this one the best because it recalls a jigsaw puzzle I was once given to while away the hours on board ship, in the days when going 'on leave' to England meant a longish sea voyage lasting several weeks.

The sense of a slight slippage in time persists as one browses at Habib's Railway Bookstore whose signboard announces that it was established in 1936. Here one can change one's Singapore dollars into Malaysian ringgit and pick up a glossy magazine for the journey.

I don't know if Hassan's Railway Station Canteen has been around as long as Habib's bookstore, but he does a good line in chicken *briani*, beef *rendang, sayur lodeh* and other local favourites, while the drinks vendor deftly pours a frothy stream of *teh tarik* into a glass from on high, like a magician performing a card trick. This is the place to take one's breakfast, prior to catching an early morning northbound train — a couple of freshly-made *roti pratha*, or *roti canai* as they are called in Malaysia, a mug of strong coffee sweetened with condensed milk and a copy of the *New Straits Times* make the perfect start to a journey. Actually, Hassan's is not a bad spot for a bite to eat even if one is not about to board a train — the station location creates its own singular ambience that offers a welcome respite from the relentless uniformity of the ubiquitous food court and hawker centre to which we normally are accustomed.

On the platform itself, the huge cast-iron buffers marking the end of the line belong to another age and behind them someone has planted a charming little garden, complete with an ornamental pool stocked with carp. I particularly like the detailing that runs along the entablature of the platform roofs — there is something Hindu in the treatment, reminiscent of the hooded *naga*-headed antefixes one finds in classical Khmer architecture — they would have appealed to Frank Lloyd Wright during his Meso-American period.

This magnificent Art Deco building was opened by Governor Sir Cecil Clementi Smith in 1932, who declared it to be a "Terminus of world importance". The present Singaporean Government has a rather less inflated regard for the building and the single line of railway track that connects it to the Causeway. These belong to the Government of Malaysia and in terms of national sovereignty, they are rather like a malignant growth, an unwelcome foreign body festering in the heart of Singapore, joined by a silvery umbilical cord to the mainland. The Singaporean Government would like the Malaysians to shift, but they won't budge and this has been a bone of some contention in recent years.

So much for Tanjong Pagar Railway Station, but whatabout the trains and the railway line itself? The first stretch of railway to be constructed in the Malay Peninsula was an eight-mile length of track running between Port Weld and Taiping in the state of Perak. Taiping was a fairly prominent place in those days on account of the rich tin deposits in the area and can boast a number of 'firsts', including the oldest botanical gardens, the oldest museum and the oldest post office in Malaysia. The Taiping railway, which was completed in June 1885, was never more than a branch line running between the Taiping town and Port Weld on the coast, but it did encourage the building of a second rail link between Klang and Kuala Lumpur, which subsequently played an important role in KL's emergence as the leading metropolis in the Peninsula.

The Klang to Kuala Lumpur railway, which was all of twenty-three miles in length, was completed in 1886. Its very first passengers were Sir Frederick Weld, K.C.M.G., accompanied by Sultan Abdul Samad. Weld was Governor of the Straits Settlements (comprising Penang, Singapore and Malacca) and had cut the first sod back in July 1883, while Sultan Abdul Samad was the paramount ruler of the state of Selangor within whose domain both Klang and Kuala Lumpur then lay. These most eminent personages boarded the train at Klang, the royal capital, and disembarked at Kuala Lumpur just over one-and-a-half hours later. The first part of the journey was taken at a leisurely pace because the ballast for the track had yet to be laid down. Further along the line, however, the engine driver worked up a good head of steam and the train and its distinguished passengers fairly whizzed along. In the words of the *Straits Times* correspondent who went along for the ride, as the train "... neared Kuala Lumpur the speed was greatly accelerated and we were going at about 30 miles an hour". I'm not sure that trains in the Malaysia travel all that much faster today, but certainly the dignitaries back then were impressed — according to the *Straits Times*, the octogenarian Sultan pronounced it to be quite the best bullock cart ride he had ever taken.

After the Kuala Lumpur-Klang line was up and running, attention was turned to completing the final link that would connect KL with the coast. The biggest headache was spanning the Klang River which required the construction of a fairly substantial bridge. After that, it was downhill all the way to Port Swettenham and with the completion of this section of the line in 1889, the first major step in providing a railway network for the whole Peninsula had been taken. The main objective, of course, was to link up the principal towns on the West Coast of the Peninsula — George Town, Taiping, Ipoh, and Kuala Lumpur — with Singapore, but branch lines to the East Coast and other destinations were also on the agenda. The grand scheme progressed incrementally, with a few miles of track being built at a time, each successive rail head, or 'end of steel' (*ujung besi*), providing a stepping stone for the next phase of construction.

The Singapore section of the line was completed in 1903, at a cost of nearly two million dollars. One of the chief arguments in favour of its construction was that apart from providing easy access to the other side of the island for travellers heading north to the Malay States, it would also encourage people to live further away from the centre of town, making the latter less congested. In this last respect the railway line seems to have been at least a qualified success with 223 persons holding season tickets in 1907.

The terminus was located at Tank Road, from where the track headed eastwards to Cuppage Road (today's Cuppage Terrace), before turning north behind Orchard Road, across Monk's Hill and on to Newton Circus. The line then followed the Bukit Timah Road to Bukit Timah Village, before finally ending up at Woodlands. At the time of its completion, the Causeway had yet to be built and so passengers were conveyed across the Johor Straits by steam ferry. When they got to the other side there was no connecting link with the mainline north until 1909, due to prevarications on the part of the Sultan of Johor who was disinclined to allow a railway line to pass through his territory. This slight inconvenience in travel arrangements did not, however, deter the authors of that splendid compendium, *Twentieth Century Impressions of British Malaya,* which appeared in 1908, from proudly announcing that "In no direction has the beneficent result of British influence in Malaya been more strikingly manifest than in the opening up of the territory, with all its rich commercial possibilities, to the outer world by the introduction of rapid means of communication between the important tin mining and agricultural centres and the coast."

And it was indeed a remarkable achievement, given that much of the Malay Peninsula at the turn of the century was either covered in primary rainforest or else was a swampy and malarial bog. The men who surveyed and then built the first railway line were heroic characters, with colourful backgrounds in the great pioneering tradition. The first General Manager of the railway in Singapore, for example, was a Mr. William Teale. Born in Ealing in 1852, he was educated in Paris and then went to the West Indies where he was engaged as a sugar planter for three years. On his return to England he took up an appointment as a clerk in the traffic office of the Great Northern Railway Company in Leeds. Unsurprisingly, this was not much to his liking, hence his removal to Singapore, where he found the life to be much more agreeable.

Teale's counterpart in Kuala Lumpur, Mr. Charles Edwin Spooner, who hailed from Hafod Tanycraig, in north Wales, was also a man of many parts. As well as being General Manager and Chief Engineer of the Federated Malay States Railways, Spooner was a big game hunter, polo player and gifted amateur artist who was responsible for designing the emblem which adorned the mail cars — a tiger springing out of the jungle at sundown. The authors of *Twentieth Century Impressions* described the image as "... very appropriate in character, as well as vigorous in its execution." This logo could be seen on the side of the mail wagon until quite recently and may even be still in use today. Spooner also found time to design the first FMSR offices in Kuala Lumpur (no longer extant).

Some idea of the kind of hardships faced by the men who actually surveyed the line is provided by Carveth Wells in his account of life as a railway engineer in Peninsular Malaya at the time of the First World War.

The newly-arrived Wells was set to work on the East Coast line, blazing a trail through the forests just north of Tembeling; here he describes his first day of surveying in the jungles of Pahang:

> I had expected to do that quarter of a mile's work in about half an hour, but it actually took me five hours and ... I reached camp late in the afternoon, burnt red as a lobster, dirty, and smarting from the bites of numerous insects, with blood running out of my boots from over-gorged leeches in my socks.

More life-threatening adversities were to come — marauding tigers, poisonous snakes, deadly swarms of wasps and flash floods among them — but Wells took them in his stride as he laconically recalls in his *Six Years in the Malay Jungle* (1925).

There is not much real jungle left in the Malay Peninsula these days and one of the sadder sights one can see is a line of open wagons, stacked high with felled forest giants, standing in the sidings of a railway station in Johor, Pahang or any of the other states where there is still a bit of primary forest left to be raped. Up until the 1970s, however, there was an awful lot of jungle around and wild animals to go with it. The story of the elephant that derailed a train has often been told, but for those who haven't heard it before, the incident occurred on the evening of the 17th September 1894, on the branch line running between Ipoh and Telok Anson. Legend has it that a wild bull elephant, believing his herd to be threatened by a monstrous new breed of armour-plated, fire-breathing pachyderm, charged a Telok Anson-bound train. The locomotive and tender were derailed, but sadly at the expense of the courageous tusker's own life. His gallant action was not forgotten, however, and a commemorative plaque was erected at the spot and still stands, I believe, over one hundred years later.

*

One would be extremely unlikely to encounter a herd of wild elephants beside the railway today, but the main line still goes through some fairly remote areas, especially between Gua Musang and Kuala Kerai, on the way to Kota Bahru. On this stretch one passes through spectacular limestone outcrops and the forest comes right down to the edge of the tracks. It always seemed to me that the train moved more slowly along this section of line — possibly for fear of fallen trees or shades of that old bull elephant near Telok Anson. There was also a perceptible drop in temperature and one could sense a certain freshness in the air, while from the forest came a steady 'zing' of cicadas, punctuated by the rhythmic 'ke-lunk, ke-lunk' of the carriage bogies passing over the joints in the track.

The older carriages had little balconies at either end, with wrought-iron balusters and hand rails, like one sees in cowboy movies. Shaded from the sun by an overhanging roof, these provided the perfect observation platform from which to enjoy the passing scenery. At country stations, the carriages would be swamped by a motley crew of itinerant food vendors who would ride the train to the next halt before jumping off to wait for another one going in the opposite direction. '*Nasi lemak, nasi lemak*', 'Curry puff, curry puff', '*Es manis*' (ice lollies) would be the cry as they passed up and down carriages. Freshly roasted peanuts, sticky green cakes made from *agar agar* seaweed-jelly and glutinous rice wrapped in *pandan* leaves — all kinds of delicacies were on offer. Not to mention the fruit — whatever was in season — mangoes, mangosteens, rambutan, bananas and of course the celebrated durian — the pungent aroma of the 'king of fruits' mingling with the stench of overflowing lavatories, is not easily forgotten and one made every effort to secure a seat as far as possible from the latter offence when embarking upon a rail journey of any length.

And if you hadn't already stuffed yourself on these rail-side attractions long before it came to dinner time, there was always the *makan* car. I have a vivid memory of travelling on the overnight train from Kuala Lumpur to Singapore, and making my way to the dining car to be confronted by an amazing spectacle. There stood a huge Chinese fellow in singlet and shorts, vigorously stirring a massive, soot-blackened *wok*, the sparks flying out the window as we hurtled through the dark Malayan night. Like some fabulous Vulcan at his forge, he effortlessly conjured up a continuous flow of *kuey teow, mee goreng, nasi goreng,* — "Any kind of *goreng* you want, Lah" — spiced with chillies and garnished with fresh coriander. Food never tasted so good, especially when accompanied by a frosty bottle of Tiger Beer, which said Vulcan pulled from a zinc bath full of ice at his feet. Actually, the train seldom sped, let alone hurtled, but somehow it seemed that way when the darkness of the night outside and the rush of air through the open windows created an illusion of speed far in excess of the thirty or so miles an hour that was the normal velocity of the Midnight Express.

Which reminds me, the trains in those days had wonderful names — the 'Magic Arrow' (*Panah Sakti*) for the daytime express, and the 'North Polar Star' for its nighttime counterpart. Today, these delightful images have been superceded by far duller designations — the prosaic People's Express and the Daytime Economy. Nor is the politely-named 'Buffet Coach', a patch on the old dining car. Ah Fai and his singlet have been replaced by pretty girls in neat uniforms who serve an unappetising range of pre-cooked, half-heated, semi-edible comestibles from a microwave. The watery coffee comes with a sachet of powdered creamer, while the tea is prepared in the manner of the French, a desultory bag of Lipton's Yellow Label, floating in a Styrofoam beaker of tepid water. I don't even bother to inquire after a bottle of beer nowadays, the catering service is presumably a Muslim franchise and doesn't run to such things.

Such is progress — rail travel in the Malaysian Peninsula today is undeniably a lot smoother, quieter, cleaner and generally more punctual than in days of yore, but some of the colour has leached out of the landscape — you won't be derailed by a wild elephant and the speeding arrow that carries you along is, sadly, no longer a magic one.

OUTSTATION

◆

out·sta·tion (out'stā'shən) *a post, station or settlement in a remote or outlying area. [1835–45; OUT + STATION]*
— *Random House Webster's Unabridged Dictionary* (1997) —

The other day, I rang up a friend at his office and was informed by his secretary that he was not available — he was "outstation." Outstation! Now there's a word that has a certain resonance to it. In my friend's case it simply meant that he was not in town. Most likely he was in Tokyo, Taipei or Hong Kong — not exactly the sort of place one identifies with the dictionary entry for 'outstation,' *viz.* "a post, station, or settlement in a remote or outlying area." There was a time, however, when the word was commonplace, a time when the principal centres of civilisation in these parts were Singapore, Kuala Lumpur, Ipoh and Penang, and everywhere else was, in varying degrees, beyond the pale. In those days, a visit to the East Coast and other less travelled regions of the Malay Peninsula was indeed to be outstation; somehow the term has managed to linger on in the office-speak of modern Singapore, a quaint anachronism from a not so distant past.

'The Outstation' is also, of course, the title of a short story by Somerset Maugham, one of six devoted to the lives of English men and women in remote parts of Borneo and Malaya, which were first published together as *The Casuarina Tree* in 1926. It is a brilliant tale of two Englishmen living in an isolated outpost on the banks of some unnamed Bornean river in the state of Sembulu, a thinly disguised Sarawak. They are the only two Europeans for hundreds of miles, yet they are estranged from one another by irreconcilable differences of class and temperament, the one an inveterate snob, the other a vulgar 'colonial', that is to say, someone born and educated, not in England, but in one of England's colonies.

I won't spoil the story for those who haven't read it by revealing too much, but there is one passage which made a strong impression on me when I first read the tale at school and which has remained with me ever since. It has to do with the 'sacrament' of reading the English newspapers.

These were dispatched from England by consignment and reached the upriver settlement some six weeks after they had appeared on the newsstands in London. The relevant passage reads as follows:

> Most people living in out of the way places when the mail comes tear open impatiently their papers and taking the last ones first glance at the latest news from home. Not so Mr. Warburton. His newsagent had instructions to write on the outside of the wrapper the date of each paper he dispatched, and when the great bundle arrived Mr. Warburton looked at these dates and with his blue pencil numbered them. His head-boy's orders were to place one on the table every morning in the verandah with the early cup of tea, and it was Mr. Warburton's especial delight to break the wrapper as he sipped his tea, and read the morning paper. Every Monday morning he read the Monday Times of six weeks back, and so it went through the week. On Sunday he read the Observer. Like his habit of dressing for dinner it was a tie to civilisation. And it was his pride that no matter how exciting the news he had never yielded to the temptation of opening a paper before its allotted time.

Never yielded! Not once! Not even during the Great War, when he could have spared himself "agonies of suspense" over the final outcome of a battle or the result of some new offensive, simply by turning to a later edition. Splendid! Of such stuff are empires made! And I have a sneaking suspicion that I would do exactly the same.

Somerset Maugham is very much out of fashion these days and has been for many years, but I have always liked his short stories especially those set in Malaya and the South Pacific. As it happens I went to the same school as he and though Maugham was not particularly happy during his rather brief time there — he records the experience in his autobiographical novel *Of Human Bondage* — nevertheless this is where he chose to deposit his mortal remains. He also bequeathed his library to

118

the school and left sufficient funds for a two-storey building to be erected to house them. There were physics laboratories on the ground floor and two large rooms above lined from floor to ceiling with bookshelves containing literally thousands of volumes, the great majority bound in leather. The Maugham Library, as the building was called, was separated from my 'house' by a patch of lawn where we played croquet in the summer term. An urn, containing the author's ashes, was interred in the wall of the library that overlooked the garden and there was a grey slate plaque which bore the simple inscription 'W. Somerset Maugham 1874-1965.' When I first started wearing contact lenses and was rather anxious about putting them in correctly, I used to place one hand over each eye in turn and looking out of my study window, check that I could read the words on Maugham's memorial slab.

Somerset Maugham was writing about Singapore and Malaya in the 1920s and according to my grandmother, and many others for that matter, he was a none too popular figure at Raffles after the first of his tales about dissipated district officers and unfaithful wives started to appear — the mere transposition of names and places was insufficient to disguise the real-life identity of the characters who appeared on the written page and there were many who were at first mortified and then incensed by the recognition of their compromised selves. So much water has passed under the bridges of the Singapore River since then and today his stories seem as historically remote as Jane Austen or Charles Dickens. In the late 1950s and early '60s, though, Maugham was still alive and the life that he described in his laconic prose lingered on in the lost margins of a dismantled Empire.

Naturally, many of Maugham's stories featured rubber planters and there were plenty of those still around at the time I am writing about here. In Maugham's day, every second rubber planter seems to have been a professional dipsomaniac or as the anonymous author of *Up and Down the China Coast* (1936) memorably put it: "Those who have never been there like to think of the Far East as steeped in the Spirit of Romance. Actually the Spirit is whisky."

No doubt the monotony of the job combined with the social isolation of the rubber planter, had a lot to do with it. Often the rubber planter lived at several hours', if not days', remove from the nearest town or outpost of civilisation, which meant that his life was almost entirely bound to the estate. Moreover, each day was more or less the same, relieved only by the alternation of dry and rainy seasons. It started well before dawn, with a roll-call of the rubber tappers — largely indentured Tamil labourers from southern India and the Jaffna Peninsula of Sri Lanka. This was then followed by endless rounds of inspection — of the estate itself, of the smoke house where the raw rubber (latex) was cured, of the labour lines and estate hospital. Then came brunch, which I had always thought to be an American invention until browsing through my collected Somerset Maugham stories whilst researching this article, where I came across the following line: "... the substantial meal, half breakfast and half luncheon, which in Borneo is called brunch." This would seem to indicate a more local origin for this term — *Webster's* simply gives a date for its first appearance (1895-1900). Brunch was followed by a longish siesta, naturally stretched out in a planter's chair on the verandah, and then three or four hours' paper work in the estate office before the day began in earnest with a 'sundowner' or three, either back at the bungalow, or, if the local society of rubber planters was so blessed, down at the club.

It was a seven-day week and tours of duty in the East were long — between three and five years, before home leave. Matrimony was usually frowned upon, if not ruled out altogether, by the big rubber companies until at least one tour had been completed. Not that the ruling made much difference — nubile European girls were as rare as hen's teeth outside of Singapore, Penang and Kuala Lumpur before the last war. Inevitably, then, whisky and native women were the solace of many a young rubber planter in the East and though both were freely indulged in and covertly accepted by the rubber planting fraternity, neither drunkenness nor a local mistress was admissible in polite society — naturally there are any number of Maugham stories involving one or other, if not both, these dissipations.

After the Second World War, the situation was rather different as improved roads and better communications rapidly opened up the country, while a new generation of young men, fresh from Europe, ushered in a changed horizon of social values and proprieties. Even so, one didn't have to travel very far along a dusty estate road to enter a twilight zone beneath the spreading rubber trees, where the old ways had yet to be replaced by the new and where one could still find a character or two straight from the pages of *The Trembling of a Leaf* (another collection of Maugham's Eastern stories, which appeared in 1921). Here are my recollections of one such figure.

In the 1960s my father kept a boat at Port Klang (or Port Swettenham as it was known then) — a 45-foot gaff-rigged pilot cutter, built at the turn of the century, with a teak mast and canvass sails. Among those who regularly joined us for our Sunday sailing parties, was a rubber planter.

He was a bluff Yorkshireman — actually he may have been from Lancashire, the qualifying adjective still stands — not bad looking in a rugged kind of way, with dark, straight hair, nice eyes, a robust constitution and large, practical hands, the sort of hands that are good at fixing mechanical things. He could have been a rugby prop-forward, but I suspect his inclination would have been more towards cricket — one could imagine him as an opening bat for Yorkshire, a might-have-been Geoff Boycott lost amongst the rubber trees. And he was quietly shy, attentive to the ladies, but with a slightly awkward manner, no doubt arising from a certain unfamiliarity with feminine ways and perspectives.

One Sunday, Desmond (not his real name) quite unexpectedly invited my mother and a woman friend of hers, Doreen, who also came sailing on regular basis, to tea at his house the following week. There was nothing untoward in this — I think he felt he'd long enjoyed their hospitality, and in particular the lavish curry tiffins which they dished up each week on board the boat, and surmised that some kind of reciprocity was in order. Whatever his motivations, the invitation was issued and accepted and a time and date agreed upon — I was roped in as a token male representative to escort the female visitors.

On the appointed day and at the appointed hour, we presented ourselves at the entrance to Desmond's rubber estate, a little to the south of the trunk road between Kuala Lumpur and Port Swettenham, and quite near to where the international airport at Subang would later be built. Desmond was there, waiting for us behind the wheel of a battered Land Rover, in order to guide us to his house which was a couple of miles from the main gate.

The estate road followed the contours of the land, winding round gentle hills and through shallow valleys. On either side, the serried ranks of rubber trees seemingly stretched away to infinity, each receding avenue a vaulted nave of foliage disappearing into a mysterious sylvan gloom of dappled light and shade. The floor of this unnatural forest lay beneath a carpet of fallen leaves, dry as parchment, but every so often one came to a fern-bordered stream or watercourse, spanned by a wooden bridge which clattered noisily as our motor cars passed over it.

Now and then we emerged from this crepuscular world of branches, leaves and tree trunks, to be dazzled by the brilliance of a sunny afternoon beneath a bright blue sky. This was where a 'section' had been cleared for new planting: the old trees felled to provide fuel for the smoke house, the remaining stumps and brushwood put to the torch to return their carbon content to the poor laterite soils. This is how the Western Front must have looked that first spring after the end of the Great War, a treeless landscape, but with the blackened stumps of a shell-shattered woodland poking through a ground cover of brilliant green vetches, the lightly-worn mantle of returning life.

Eventually we came to Desmond's house, a single-storey bungalow set on a slight eminence, with the rubber trees coming right up to the very edge of the verandah. We parked our car beside his Land Rover and followed Desmond up the steps. The interior was Spartan and little more than one might have expected — the dingy walls in need of a coat of paint, the ubiquitous suite of cane furniture, a teak dinning room table with chairs to match, a selection of bottles standing on the sideboard in various states of plenitude. There was also a framed photograph of a school cricket eleven, the mount discoloured by a watermark, and a selection of photogravures of Classical scenes hung at various strategic points around the room — quite possibly they had been there since the turn of the century, successively bequeathed to each new occupant of the bungalow like some sacred patrimony, a civilising influence in a heathen land.

I went outside to explore the exciting terrain and to gather fallen rubber nuts, their richly burnished outer shell, flecked like chocolate quail's eggs. Slowly, I worked myself round to the back of the house and as I was poking around in the leaves with a stick I became aware of someone watching me. Looking up, I saw a young Chinese woman staring at me from the window of the kitchen, which together with the servants' quarters was detached from the rest of the bungalow. She met my gaze for a brief instant and then turned away to busy herself within. I continued my reconnaissance. The dead leaves crackled underfoot and the odd lizard or skink, the same dry colour as the leaves, scurried away at my approach; my pockets bulged with rubber nuts.

A call summoned me to tea which was brought through on a tray by the young Chinese woman I had previously seen. We sat on the verandah, of course. My mother and her friend, cool in their crisp, cream-coloured linen dresses, reclined languidly in their rattan chairs, while Desmond, perched nervously on the edge of his, poured the tea with as much grace as he could muster.

Everything was laid out very correctly. There was a paper doily on the tea tray and a proper tea service — blue-and-white Delftware, a little chipped, but with a full complement of cups and saucers, a sugar bowl with cubed sugar and electroplated tongs, and a milk jug. Desmond apologised for the condensed milk, but the local Chinese provision shop did not stock the bottled Fernleaf variety imported from New Zealand which was our substitute for fresh milk in those days. Never mind, the spread was munificent — cucumber sandwiches, potted shrimp paste, a huge pomelo, and slices of mango and watermelon on a bed of ice cubes. Last but not least, there was a magnificent home-made sponge cake with real jam filling. Not a bad effort, we thought, for a lonely bachelor in the back of beyond. And then something rather curious started to happen.

From the kitchen at the back of the bungalow came a loud crash of breaking crockery. Evidently someone had dropped a stack of dinner plates. No matter, accidents will happen, we resumed our conversation. A minute or so later there was another smash of porcelain from the kitchen. Bad luck! Twice in one day. At the third crash Desmond excused himself and hastily disappeared towards the back of the house. He reappeared a short while later.

"The *amah*," he explained with a wan smile, "bit of an off day, y'know?" The end of his sentence was punctuated by the sound of yet more disintegrating china. Desmond winced.

"Come on," said my mother, rather briskly. "I think it's time we were off; it's quite a long drive back to KL and it's beginning to get dark." Crash!

We thanked Desmond for his lovely tea party, declined his kind offer to escort us back to the main road, and made as rapid a retreat to our car as was decently possible whilst affecting not to hear the sounds of disintegrating china which continued to emanate from the kitchen wing. The shadows were indeed lengthening and the closeness of the surrounding rubber trees increased the preternatural gloom of the place. Desmond waved farewell from the steps of his verandah and then, as our car rounded the bend in his driveway, slowly turned and went inside. We drove some way in thoughtful silence, before I posed the question that was on everyone's mind: "Mummy, why did Desmond's *amah* break his plates?"

"Oh, I think she rather likes Uncle Desmond," was her somewhat baffling reply. Somehow I knew better than to pursue the issue any further at that moment in time, though I thought that hurling a dinner service at the wall was a strange way to demonstrate one's affection for another person, let alone one's employer. Clearly some other factor was involved, but for the moment I couldn't be sure just what it was, so I just settled myself in the back seat of the car instead, while my mother and Doreen chatted about other things all the way back to KL.

It was some weeks before Desmond joined us again for our Sunday sail. He was his usual self, shy but friendly, and happy to have a large, second-helping of curried chicken which he said he'd missed. Naturally I was keen to hear more about the broken crockery and to know whether he ended up with any plates left to eat his dinner off, but strangely the incident was never once mentioned. Nor were we ever invited to tea on his estate again.

15th FEBRUARY, 1942

The possibility of Singapore having no landward defences no more entered into my mind than that of a battleship being launched without a bottom.

— Winston Churchill, *The Second World War* (1951) —

When I was a child, I used to live in a house off Braddell Road, which was considered distinctly *ulu* in those days, *ulu* being the Malay word for the headwaters of a river or stream and signifying, in this context, a place that was up country, in the wilds, at the back of beyond. And so it was, in a manner of speaking, at least in relation to the centre of town. Our neighbours were *kampong* folk who reared pigs and poultry for the market place; the countryside round about was given over to vegetable farms and commercial fishponds; and the main road was bordered not by pavements and curb stones, but bamboo hedgerows and muddy ditches. At night, the stars shone bright in the absence of street lights and the hustle and bustle of downtown Singapore seemed a long way off.

Clearly, an expedition to the Cold Storage on Orchard Road was not something to be embarked upon lightly, especially in the days before my mother learnt to drive, but no matter, there was a row of shop houses nearby which provided most of the necessities of daily life from the proverbial sealing wax to a ball of string. And in one of these provision stores, there was a boy — an *ang mo* boy in his late 'teens — who served behind the counter and who spoke not a word of English, though he could converse with local customers in fluent Hokkien or Cantonese. Naturally, my mother was very curious to know how a European boy came to be working in this shop, the apparent adopted son of its Chinese owner, so she asked Ah Jong, our black and white Cantonese *amah* to make some discrete enquiries in this connection. The story was as follows:

One day, shortly before the fall of Singapore to the Japanese in February 1942, the shopkeeper, found a European baby crying in the rubble of a bombed-out house which had received a direct hit in a recent air-raid. There was no sign of the parents — he presumed them to be lying dead beneath the smouldering wreckage — and so the good man scooped up the bawling infant and carried him back to his young wife. Although the shopkeeper tried to find out the identity of the boy and trace other members of his family, both at the time and after the war, no one came forward to claim the child — what relatives he may have had overseas no doubt assumed he had been killed in the bombing raid that had claimed his parents' lives — and so the shopkeeper and his wife raised him as one of their own children. His first words were spoken in their dialect and he went to the local school together with his Chinese 'brothers' and 'sisters,' which is why he never got to learn English. At the time that we came to live at Braddell Heights he would have been about sixteen years old; today, he would be approaching sixty. I wonder what happened to him.

On February 15th of this year [2000], it will be the 58th anniversary of the fall of Singapore to the Japanese, a catastrophic event for the peoples of this island — not only the European community, but also for the native Malays, and the Chinese and Indian populace too. Winston Churchill described the surrender as "the worst disaster and the largest capitulation in British military history." Of the 140,000 odd British and Commonwealth soldiers involved in the campaign to defend Malaya and Singapore, 9,000 lost their lives, some managed to get away and a staggering 130,000 were taken prisoner. On the eve of the surrender, General Tomoyuki Yamashita, commander of the Japanese forces, had only 30,000 men at his disposal, having lost 3,500 men during the previous six weeks' campaign. He was therefore outnumbered three to one and he was also running low on ordnance, but with his tough demands for an immediate and unconditional surrender he managed to bluff his way to victory over the demoralised Allies.

In a disaster of this magnitude it is natural to look around for a scapegoat, someone to point the finger at, and there are plenty to hand, among them Governor Sir Miles Shenton Thomas and Lieutenant-General

A. E. Percival, General Officer Commanding Malaya (April 1941-February 1942). It is the latter who is usually singled out as the principal recipient of blame, perhaps a little unfairly, as authors Richard Holmes and Anthony Kemp point out in their excellent *The Bitter End: The Fall of Singapore 1941-42*:

> An obvious candidate for the unattractive post of scapegoat, Percival was no 'character' who went down in a last stand yelling defiance at his enemy. Rather, he was a sober staff officer who weighed up the situation and decided to surrender rather than cause appalling — and probably pointless — suffering, especially to the Asian citizens of Singapore.

But if in the end Percival's decision to surrender was the right one, there can be no doubt that many of his previous actions and preparations to defend Singapore were decidedly odd, even without the benefit of hindsight. In particular, his notorious refusal to authorise the construction of defences along the north coast of the island on the grounds that it would be bad for morale was extraordinary, especially in view of the fact that this pronouncement came on Boxing Day 1941, when Penang, Ipoh and Kuala Lumpur had already fallen to the Japanese in their lightning advance down the Malay Peninsula.

But I do not intend to give a history lesson here. The story of the fall of Singapore is still a contentious subject and the rights or wrongs of who did this, or didn't do that, are too many and too complex to do justice tothose concerned in an article of a few thousand words. Feelings run deep and I would run the risk of causing grave offence to many parties if I were to treat so serious a debate in a superficial manner. If, however, one were to make some general observations without pointing a finger at anyone in particular, I think it would be fair to say that perhaps the biggest single contributory cause to the fall of Singapore was one of attitude. There was this idea — quite unfounded as it turned out — that Singapore was an impregnable fortress. Put a little more bluntly, the British military simply could not believe that the island could be overrun by what was perceived, in the crudest of caricatures, to be an army of bow-legged little men with buck teeth and defective eyesight.

There were other weaknesses too, most notably the poor communications that existed between different branches of the military and between the military and the civil administration, but ultimately it was the complete underestimation of Japan as a fighting force, combined with the idea 'Fortress Singapore' was nigh on impregnable, which ultimately changed the course of history in this part of the world. When the British returned, victorious, to Singapore, after a three-and-a-half year absence, they may have been cheered by those whom they liberated, but their prestige in the region had suffered a mortal blow and they came back more as caretakers than as overlords.

At the outbreak of the war in the Far East, Singapore's military defences rested primarily on a series of coastal batteries spread along the island's seaward shores. 'Fortress Changi', which comprised a battery of heavy artillery and anti-aircraft guns, defended the eastern sea approaches to the new naval base in the Johor Straits, while the western approaches to Singapore, were covered by Fort Silosa, on the island of Pulau Blakang Mati (Sentosa), and the Labrador battery at the entrance to Keppel Harbour. The only problem was that when the Japanese invaded, they came not from the sea but overland, across the Causeway from Johor, having first overrun the entire Malay Peninsula in a dazzling campaign that left the British military in complete disarray. This has given rise to the popular story that the reason why Singapore fell so quickly was the fact that all the guns were pointing in the wrong direction in anticipation of a seaborne invasion that never came. While there is some truth in this, it so happens that most of the seaward-facing ordnance could actually be turned about to fire inland. No, the real problem was that the batteries were equipped with armour-piercing shells, intended to be used against battleships and troop carriers, rather than the high-explosive shells needed for effect against land forces when the Japanese began to assemble on the shores of the Johor Straits prior to crossing the Causeway.

Another critical factor was that there were not enough anti-aircraft guns to prove effective against the waves of Japanese bombers that blasted Singapore night and day in the weeks leading up to the invasion. Nor were there enough aircraft to engage the Japanese in the skies, and those that were available were old and verging on the obsolescent. The principal fighter-plane at the RAF's disposal, was the American-built Buffalo, which Air Chief-Marshall, Sir Robert Brooke-Popham, Commander-in-Chief Far East, assured everyone were "quite good enough for Malaya." Not everyone was convinced, but when the Navy asked the Chiefs-of-Staff for some Hurricanes to be sent to the Far East, some six months before war broke out, they were told by the Vice-Chief of the Air Staff that the Buffalo fighters "would be more than a match for the Japanese aircraft which were not of the latest type." As it happened, it was the Buffalo that was no match for the Japanese Zeroes, which were speedier, could climb faster, had a higher ceiling and generally were more manoeuvrable in every way. When, in the end, some fifty-odd Hurricanes were shipped to the RAF in Singapore, they were found on arrival to be minus their propellers — no saboteur could have rendered them inoperable more effectively.

The fact that much of Singapore's supposed military strength might be more apparent than real, did not go unnoticed, but even then the alarm bells failed to ring. According to C-in-C Brooke-Popham, "the greatest value of Singapore was the illusion of impregnability built up in the Japanese mind." In actual fact, the illusion was more in the minds of the British than their Japanese opponents who for years had been building up intelligence about the strategic defences of Singapore and were very well aware of the island's relative strengths and weaknesses.

In 1940 there were some 8,000 Japanese citizens resident in Malaya and Singapore, a large number of whom seemed to have lived a double life as agents working on behalf of the Japanese military. More than half of this expatriate Japanese population were living here in Singapore where, prior to the war, there were a great many Japanese shops and businesses located in Middle Road. There were also numerous Japanese doctors and dentists, as well as a large number of Japanese brothel owners, not to mention the ubiquitous Japanese photographer. Together they assembled a formidable body of knowledge about the topography and civil and military infrastructure of Singapore which was sent back to Japan to be collated by military intelligence. Senior Japanese military strategists even visited Singapore as tourists and were shown around the island, enabling them to make their own assessments of military installations, communication services, possible landing sites and so on. It was also later revealed that Mr. Mimatsu, the semiofficial photographer to the armed forces in Singapore, had served in the Japanese army as a colonel in World War I and had been sent to Singapore to gather as much information as he could about British defences! In fact, at the outbreak of war the Japanese probably had a much better grasp of the military situation in Singapore than the British Chiefs-of-Staff.

Inadequate provisions for the war against Japan may have reflected a certain naivete on the part of the military, but it also revealed a more pernicious line of thinking which ultimately fed on deeply entrenched British assumptions of racial superiority *vis à vis* their opponents. It was popularly rumoured that Japanese pilots were myopic and their planes were made of paper and wood. It was also said that the Japanese set off firecrackers at night to frighten their enemy and that Japanese rifles were so poorly made that the bullets had to be squeezed out.

And if defective equipment and poor eyesight were not enough to constrain the Japanese, then there was always the mountainous terrain and jungles of the Malay Peninsula which were themselves considered to be a formidable line of defence against any invasion from the north. Should such an attempt be made, then clearly there would be plenty of time to send for reinforcements from India and Australia; the idea of jungle warfare simply hadn't occurred to the British High Command, or if it did they simply chose to disregard it.

But it had to the Japanese, whose soldiers were dressed in thin tropical uniforms and wore light, rubber-soled shoes on their feet. Their British counterparts, on the other hand, looked "like Christmas trees," with their heavy boots, webbing, packs and haversacks, water bottles, blankets and groundsheets— even great coats and respirators. They could hardly walk, much less fight. As Shell engineer, Gerald Scott, recalled some some forty years after the event: "We didn't believe that the Japs could come through the back door in gym shoes through the jungle and knock the place sideways." But they did and what is more, when they got to a road they jumped on bicycles and sped on their way in parties of forty or fifty, riding three or four abreast. But I am getting ahead of myself.

The first bombs fell on Singapore at around four o'clock in the morning on Monday, 8th December. This was just a few hours after Japanese troops had started to come ashore at Kota Bahru, at twenty five minutes after midnight, and less than an hour and a half after the bombs had begun to fall on Pearl Harbour (because Hawaii was on the other side of the International Date Line, it was eight o'clock on the morning of December 7th there). Although Japan's entry into the war had long been anticipated, many people had such faith in the security of Fortress Singapore that they thought the raid was just another practice drill. The city lights were all lit up and continued to blaze throughout the attack, guiding the enemy planes to their targets, because liaison between the army and the civil authorities was so poor that no one could find the man with the key to the power house to turn them off. Chinatown was the worst hit and when the aeroplanes departed, they left 61 people dead and a further 133 injured.

The *Straits Times* editorial for the morning of that same day read: "War has come to Malaya. Let it be stated at once that the situation is well in hand. There is no cause for panic ... ." By midnight, however, the RAF airfield at Kota Bahru had fallen to the Chrysanthemum Division of the 25th Imperial Japanese Army under the command of General Tomoyuki Yamashita, and the advance on Singapore had begun.

On the evening after the first Japanese bombing raid over Singapore, His Majesty's Ships, the *Prince of Wales* and the *Repulse* set sail from the naval base at Sembawang and headed for the east coast of Malaya. The *Repulse* had been built in 1915, but the *Prince of Wales* was a modern man-of-war and like the *Titanic*, was reputed to be unsinkable. But without air cover — the aircraft carrier HMS *Indomitable* which was meant to have accompanied them to the Far East had run aground off Jamaica — they were sitting targets and their crew as good as shark-bait. Two days later they lay at the bottom of the South China Sea with 845 men drowned. Apparently the British at that time thought that the Japanese Zero fighter plane had a range of 200 miles; in actual fact it was 1000 miles which enabled them to operate from airfields in Indo-China.

The loss of the two great ships was a devastating blow. Churchill was informed by the First Sea Lord of the disaster on the morning of 10th December, and recalling this moment later, wrote: "I put the telephone down. I was thankful to be alone. In all the war I never received a more direct shock."

Within a week the Japanese had overrun an undefended Penang without taking a single Japanese casualty. The secret evacuation of the European population from Penang just before the Japanese got there, naturally resulted in an enormous loss of British prestige in the eyes of local people, who were unable to leave the island. Their disappointment and feeling of betrayal was exacerbated when shortly afterwards the Rt. Hon. Sir Alfred Duff Cooper, who was Churchill's special envoy to the Far East, gave a broadcast in which he stated that "It has been necessary to evacuate many of the civilian population," adding that "We can only be thankful that so many people have been safely removed." He was, of course, referring mainly to the European community and his insensitivity to the fate of Penang's Asian population was glaringly obvious. Here in Singapore, Governor Shenton Thomas was furious at Duff Cooper's lack of tact and summoned the leaders of the Malay, Chinese and Indian communities to apologise. But the damage was done, the colonial masters were masters no more and their assurances that they would defend the peoples of Malaya against the enemy, no matter what the cost, were revealed to be hollow — the Malayan campaign later came to be known locally, as *tarek orang puteh lari,* 'the time the white men ran.'

Ironically, the coverage of the Malayan campaign in the press and government communiques over the next few weeks gave the impression that the British were actually doing rather well in the fight against the invaders. The Japanese were always reported to be suffering "heavy losses" and their advance was being "hampered" at every turn. The British retreat was not a rout but a "strategic withdrawal" and so on. But the Japanese had air superiority and with the sinking of the *Prince of Wales* and the *Repulse,* they also had the freedom of the seas. Kuala Lumpur fell on 11ᵗʰ January, yet even at that late hour there was still tremendous confidence that even if the Japanese overran the Malay Peninsula, they would never be able to take Fortress Singapore — one month before the fall of Singapore, passenger liners were still leaving Singapore with plenty of berths available.

By mid-January 1942, the population of Singapore town, which was normally some 550,000, had swollen to one million. And every day, there came the Japanese bombers. On Tuesday 20ᵗʰ January, for example, eighty-one enemy aircraft came over the city in three waves, flying high above the barrage of anti-aircraft fire — "like silver fish floating in a blue sea" — with not a single British plane in the sky to intercept them.

Incredibly, some semblance of normal civilian life continued. There were still afternoon teas at Robinson's, which in those days was a large department store in Raffles Place, and dances at the Raffles Hotel. Even as late as January 1942, one still had to book a table at Raffles despite the almost nightly bombing raids — the hotel engineer sat up on the roof with a whistle: four blasts signalled the approach of incoming enemy aircraft. The Singapore Swimming Club, out at Tanjong Rhu, also remained a popular place for lunch which was served on its broad verandah from where one could watch daytime bombing-raids on the docks.

Between 16th and 24th January, there was fierce fighting involving Australian and Indian troops in the area of Muar and Yong Peng on the West Coast of the Peninsula. Ultimately the Japanese prevailed and on 26th January, Percival gave the orders for a complete withdrawal to Singapore. On the morning of the 31st January, the last of the British forces on the mainland, the Argyll and Sutherland Highlanders, crossed the Causeway marching to the skirl of their bagpipes playing 'Hieland Laddie' and shortly afterwards a seventy yard breach was blown in the Causeway. The following day, the Japanese began shelling Singapore.

Although there was no official order from Governor Thomas to evacuate women and children — it was felt that it would lower British prestige — the time had clearly come for the final reckoning. The choice was quite simple — either get out or else remain and face internment by the Japanese and all that this might entail; there were queues half a day long outside the P&O manager's bungalow in Cluny Road, where the shipping line's offices had been moved in order to escape from the bombing downtown.

My great-uncle, who was a High Court Judge, was urged to leave Singapore on one of the last ships as he was certain to suffer horribly at the hands of the Japanese, having sentenced more than one Japanese photographer to death for spying. The ship and its entire complement of crew and passengers sailed from the docks at Tanjong Pagar and were never seen or heard of again.

Not everyone who could have got away chose to do so. There were wives who decided to stick by their husbands, no matter what the consequences, and others who felt that to leave would be like running away and a betrayal of the Asian peoples of Singapore who had put their trust in the British as their protectors.

They didn't have long to learn their fate, for on Saturday, 7th February, crack Japanese troops from the Konoe Imperial Guards occupied Pulau Ubin as a ploy to divert attention from the main landing sites which were at Tanjong Buloh and Tanjong Murai to the west. It worked and when 20,000 Japanese troops came ashore on the northwest coast on the evening of the following day, they were met by only 2,500 men from the Australian 22nd Brigade and the members of Dalforce, a special group of local volunteers under the command of Colonel J. D. Dalley of the Malayan Special Branch. The latter included both Nationalist and Communist Chinese in their ranks, many of whom were actually in prison when Dalforce was constituted on Christmas Day, 1941 — a deal was worked out for their release if they agreed to join forces against the Japanese. When the invasion came, these local heroes fought so valiantly that they earned themselves the epithet "Dalley's Desperadoes," but in the end even they could not hold the Japanese and had to fall back.

By the next day, Monday, 9th February, the breach in the Causeway had been repaired and the Japanese Imperial Guard were crossing into Singapore. This time, however, they met with strong resistance from the Australian 27th Brigade and were about to withdraw when the guns at Kranji suddenly fell silent — the Australians had been ordered to retreat. This 'unforced error' was typical of the confusion and miscommunication that characterised the final stand of Singapore and more were to follow. The very next day, 10th February, Lieutenant-General Percival worked out a contingency plan for a strategic withdrawal of troops to defensive positions around the edge of the city, but when commanders in the field received news of the plan they understood it to be orders for an immediate withdrawal from the front line. By the time the countermand had been given the line had been broken and Australian troops were streaming into the city.

*

The last days of Singapore before the fall, make in turn dismal, exhilarating, harrowing and uplifting reading. Again, I cannot do justice here to the extraordinary events which unfolded in the short hours and minutes that for many seemed to fill all eternity, but there are several excellent accounts available, most notably the volume by Holmes and Kemp mentioned above, Noel Barber's *A Sinister Twilight* (1968) and most recently, Lee Geok Boi's *Syonan: Singapore Under the Japanese, 1942-1945*, which was published in 1992 to commemorate the fiftieth anniversary of the fall. Massacre, rape and widespread death and destruction were the order of the day, but there were also moments of almost surreal levity in the last moments of a dying era.

They kept on dancing at the Raffles almost to the very end — the last dance was on the 12th February, just three days before the surrender, with Japanese troops already having overrun many parts of the island. Leo Jenkins, a rubber planter who had volunteered for the army at the outbreak of war, recalled the last waltz:

> I remember watching a great dance, the last that was held in the hotel before the fall of Singapore. How gay the ladies, the smiles and laughter, how beautiful the dresses and smart the white mess kits of the officers! I remember remarking to one of my companions. 'This must be just like the Duchess of Richmond's ball before the battle of Waterloo!'

The end came on the morning of 15th February, which was the first day of the Lunar New Year — the Chinese Year of the Horse. A conference was held between Percival and his commanders in the so-called 'Battle Box,' the nerve centre of British military's GHQ at Fort Canning — a hot and stuffy hole with poor air-conditioning — and the decision was taken to surrender. The meeting ended at 11.15 A.M. whereupon a deputation set out for the Japanese lines to arrange a meeting with General Yamashita. They drove along Bukit Timah Road with a big white flag flying until they could go no further and then proceeded on foot. Later that same day came the long walk to the Ford Factory, the moment of total defeat captured in the famous black and white photograph of Percival and his aides — Brigadiers Torrance and Newbiggin, and Major Cyril Wild — in flapping, knee-length shorts and tin helmets, carrying a huge Union Jack and an equally enormous white flag of truce. The Union Jack was later requested by the Japanese, but the officer who was believed to have had it in his possession told them that he had "burned it that night on the ramparts of Fort Canning, looking towards England and home." In actual fact, the flag was hidden away and somehow smuggled into Changi Gaol, where it was brought out for the next three and a half years for the funerals of British and Australian POWs.

Surrender terms were signed at 6.10 that evening. According to the diary of his ADC, Yamashita apparently wanted to pass on a few kind words to the defeated Percival, pale-faced and red-eyed through lack of sleep, but he said nothing because he did not speak English and "he realised how difficult it is to convey heartfelt sympathy when the words are being interpreted by a third person."

The papers signed, Percival returned to GHQ at Fort Canning and sent his last message to General Wavell, C-in-C ABDA (American, British, Dutch, Australian) Command:

> Owing to losses from enemy action, water, petrol, food and ammunition practically finished. Unable therefore to continue the fight any longer. All ranks have done their best and are grateful for your help.

"There after," concludes the *Official History of the War Against Japan*, "all communication with Singapore ceased." And at 8.30 that same evening, the guns at last fell silent.

EAST OF SUEZ

The postcard reads:

21st May

Well here we are on our way — it's lonely & warm & we are now wearing summer clothes. I am coping quite well with J & everyone is very kind. We had our first dance last night, the Captain also gave a cocktail party beforehand. We are going at a good speed. We have been passing the N. African coast all day. The sea is wonderful. Will write again. Much love, B.

m.s. "WILLEM RUYS"

Uitg. Fotografische Afd. "Willem Ruys" R. No. 1

20 C
NEDERLAND

Miss Doris Bertuchi
Organisation and
Training Division,
S.H.A.P.E
British Forces Post
Office 6.
FRANCE.

Such were the days, still, hot, heavy, disappearing one by one into the past, as if falling into an abyss forever open in the wake of the ship; and the ship, lonely under a wisp of smoke, held on her steadfast way black and smouldering in a luminous immensity ...

— Joseph Conrad, *Lord Jim* (1900) —

❖

There is a dark hour of the night when one wakes from a hitherto untroubled sleep to suddenly find oneself standing at the edge of the Abyss — the frightful realisation of the transient nature of this world and the seemingly inevitable fact of one's own ultimate annihilation. In a word, Oblivion! The heart misses a beat — several actually — and one experiences a sensation of falling, a fall without measure or check, rather like Alice's descent of the rabbit hole.

Sometimes I am assailed by rather similar feelings when travelling by aeroplane and I chance to reflect upon the immediate circumstances in which I find myself. Here one is, along with a couple of hundred fellow passengers and crew, sitting in little more than a cigar tube with wings, some five miles above the earth's surface, hurtling through the stratosphere at more than five hundred miles an hour with nothing either below or above but empty space. I believe that today, at any one moment in time, there are some two million of the planet's inhabitants in such a position. Two million people, at this very minute, whose lives are supported by nothing more substantial than a combination of air pressures — the propulsive thrust of a jet turbine and the uplift of an aerofoil. It really is an extraordinary accomplishment: a veritable triumph of mind over matter. No one, up until this century — with the exception of Icarus and the odd Leonardo — would have believed such a thing to be possible. To traverse the heavens was a prerogative of the gods — it is what made them different from us mere mortals and quite honestly I would much prefer that things had remained that way. Give me a tall ship and a star to steer her by any day rather than an infernal flying machine that can whizz us half way across the world and back again in a matter of hours. To travel like this leaves one with little sense of having been anywhere at all.

*

It was not until the beginning of the 1960s that the jet aircraft superceded the passenger liner as the principal means of getting around the world and I count it as my good fortune to have been in at the very end of the great era of maritime travel, the golden age of the Peninsula and Oriental Steam Navigation Company, Glenn Line, Blue Funnel, and the Rotterdam Lloyd Royal Mail. In those days, it took about six weeks to make a sea passage from England to Singapore and one really felt that one had come half way across the world when one got here. As a child, with a child's sense of time, the days at sea were beyond number — who could count them? Half the world and half a life time, or so it seemed to me, young as I was then.

The voyage would begin at Southampton under grey and drizzling skies. My impressions of this part of the journey are rather vague, wrapped in the cotton wool mists of time like the swirling fog that seemed to be an elemental feature of these departures. We would come down from London on the boat train and there would always be a bit of a party beforehand at the railway station to send us on our way. This was an invariably fairly rowdy affair fuelled by the excitement of the occasion and alcohol from the station bar. Just about everyone boarding the train was destined for the boat and all their friends and relatives had come to see them off. There were women in hats and gloves, and men in trilbies with pipes — each group of passengers had their own coterie of well-wishers gathered around them. In our case there were of course aunts and uncles, partners from the London office and friends of my parents from Palestine and the war. They all said how they envied us and how they wished they could be coming along too, and all the while in the background, the clamour and din of a great railway terminus with the minute hand on the enormous station clock sweeping towards the moment of departure.

Time to go. A whistle and the slamming of carriage doors, the window hastily pulled down for a last handshake. "Goodbye, goodbye; *bon voyage*, see you in two years' time." A flutter of handkerchiefs, the wave of a trilby, a pipe raised aloft in salute, and the train slowly pulls away from the platform. A moment's sadness at parting from loved ones, but trains are exciting and the grey suburbs of London are rushing by. Kneeling on the seats I gaze down from the elevated railway embankment on row upon row of grimy terrace houses with blackened brick facades and wet slate roofs. Tiny backyards and neglected gardens, overgrown with nettles and filled with rusting bicycles and perambulators, a tide of suburban detritus washed up on the back doorstep of civilisation. And then the sodden English countryside under a leaden sky, a last chance to gaze upon cows, green fields and muddy lanes, trees with no leaves and all the other strange and exotic topographical features that belonged to the land of the uncles and the aunts.

The Home counties gave way to Hampshire, the spires of Winchester Cathedral, the rolling downs of Eastleigh and then the noisy bustle of Southampton Docks, with the mewling cry of seagulls wheeling over head. There would be the ship at the quay side, a great wall of steel with a dozen rows of portholes blazing in the wintry gloom and a gangway leading up to a small door in the hull. Like Jonah entering the whale, one steps across the raised threshold into the throbbing, warm interior of the metal leviathan.

All ships have the same smell — a combination of metal and wood, polished brass and paint, turpentine and tar, grease and sea salt. Bright lights lead down into the belly of the beast and a steward escorts us to our cabin, shepherding us down steep flights of stairs and along corridors that make sharp right angle turns — Passenger Deck A, Passenger Deck B — would we ever find our way back again?

The cabin, at last: a door is held open for us, revealing a small but well-appointed room with bunk beds and a little wooden ladder for ascending to the upper berth. There is a minute bathroom to one side with a shower and toilet facilities, but best of all to my mind is the brass porthole set in the wall opposite. A bedroom with a porthole — fantastic!

Our metal cabin trunks, which have been sent on before us, are standing there in the middle of the floor. I recall their chunky, circular, brass locks, which are hinged and spring back on themselves when released. My Aunt Doris, though, preferred to travel with her clothes and personal effects packed into half-a-dozen wartime ammunition chests — there were some who thought this a little odd but it definitely carried a certain cachet.

A huge bunch of cut flowers sent by friends with a note wishing us a safe journey, fills the tiny room with their fragrance; my father pours himself a whiskey into a glass from the wash-hand basin. Then comes a last call for all visitors to return to shore and we go up on deck to witness our departure. It is dark now but there are plenty of people still on the quay, their white faces turned upward to the gallery of passengers that line the decks waving their last farewells. A series of blasts from the ship's sirens gives the signal to cast off. The hawsers are slipped and a crack of water opens up between the side of the ship and the dock as the tugboats take up the strain. The chorus of echoing "Goodbyes" swells to a crescendo, and then slowly dies away like the ragged cheers at a football stadium when the ball goes out of play. The distance between ship and shore increases, there is water all around us, the people on the quay are growing small. A final blast of farewell from the ship's siren and we move out into the Solent, heading for the English Channel. All departures are moments of poignancy but the sailing of a great passenger liner carrying the lives of so many across the seas to distant ports in foreign lands was a particularly moving occasion.

As I have said, I have few recollections of the first part of these voyages. No doubt the cold and inclement weather in the Channel and the Bay of Biscay kept one confined to one's cabin or the play nursery where the children on board would be deposited, while their parents got on with the important business of socialising with other passengers and securing themselves a place at the Captain's table, which was always sure to have the best food. It is only when we arrive in the Mediterranean with its sunny days and azure skies that memories are reawakened and those long ago voyages come back into focus.

The first port of call was usually Malta. The ship would put into the Grand Harbour for half a day to pick up fresh vegetables and other supplies and maybe the odd passenger. Very few people got off here — most of those on board were travelling to Africa and the Far East, for although India and Pakistan had been independent for over a decade by that time, there nevertheless remained a fair proportion of the map, east of Suez, that was still coloured pink and it was to these last outposts of Empire that the majority of our fellow passengers were heading. There were tea planters from India and Ceylon, and rubber planters from Malaya, railway engineers, school teachers, civil servants and magistrates, company men from the great agency houses — Guthries, Bousteads, Harrison and Crosfields, Sime Darby — every man and his dog was on board and heading East "to reap his old reward."

Leaving the rocky fortress island of Malta behind, the ship headed across the eastern Mediterranean for Port Said and the Suez Canal. This was the time to swap the woollen and worsted weave of winter for the cottons and linens of the tropics and on allotted days, according to a roster, passengers were allowed to go down to the trunk room where trunks that could not be accommodated in their cabins were stored, and unpack more suitable clothing for the increasingly warmer climes.

On one occasion we passed an erupting volcano at night. Mount Etna? Or was it Stromboli? This was around the time that Roberto Rosellini directed his film of the same name on the island, starkly shot in black and white and starring his beautiful wife, Ingrid Bergman. Whichever volcano it was, I remember being taken up on deck to witness the fireworks, far away on the horizon, flaring up and then dying away, like a red-hot coal, smouldering in the dark night.

Port Said has an infamy which it probably does not wholly deserve. In as far as prostitution and other such goings on are concerned I suspect it is no better or no worse than any other major sea port — wherever ships and sailors put into shore one expects to find this kind of thing and Port Said simply answered its calling. As a child I was not party to much low life anyway and my memories are more of hot and dusty boulevards, men in red, tasselled tarbooshes, snatches of Egyptian popular song — "O Mustafa, Mu'usta'afaa" — and a huge population of itinerant street vendors, roaming in a predatory fashion along the Quai du Nord and other major thoroughfares, selling just about everything imaginable from alabaster cigarette holders to the inevitable dirty postcard.

Speaking of which, the Port Said dirty postcard lives on in the popular imagination as a quintessential feature of the place and it is interesting to learn something of their history. Evelyn Waugh, describing Port Said at the end of the 1920s, writes that "The original plates of the photographs are ... of some antiquity, having been made for sale at the first International Exhibition in Paris and being brought to Port Said for the celebrations of the opening of the Suez Canal." He adds that "There have been innumerable imitations since then, of course, but it seemed to me these earlier examples left little room for improvement [though] it was interesting to observe that, for all their nudity, they are unmistakably 'dated' by [an] indefinable air of period."

For my own part, I was more taken by the stuffed leather camels of varying sizes and the *gully-gully* men and snake charmers. The *gully-gully* men were a sort of conjuror and magician rolled into one. They often were dressed in brilliantly coloured clothes, all stripes and patches, part golliwog, part Punch and Judy, part Eastern harlequin, and together with the snake charmers, they would come on board ship to entertain us children with their tricks and fancies. As far as I recall this largely consisted of drawing seemingly unending streams of brightly coloured paper 'spaghetti' from their mouths. Yards and yards of the stuff would spew forth, pulled out hand over hand. And, just when one was convinced that there could be no more, the *gully-gully* man would twist his ear, as if turning on a tap, and another fathom of ticker tape would be disgorged. We children loved it and yelled for more. If we were lucky, the *gully-gully* man, just as he reached the top of the gangway to return to shore, might pause and turning round to face us, hiccup, whereupon another ream of shredded paper would issue forth. Hilarious, we thought.

The snake charmers were good too. Turbaned and dressed in flowing robes, they sat cross-legged on the deck in front of their baskets, blowing their curious reed pipes with flared mouths like sawn-off clarinets, and swaying all the while from side to side in time with their high-pitched, warbling, wandering tune. At first nothing would happen, but the *fakir* played on and then suddenly the snake was there before our eyes! A hooded cobra, emerging from the depths of the basket and swaying too in time to the music of the pipes, forked tongue flicking, hood flared. Actually, I believe it is the motion of the snake charmer rather than his tune which hypnotises the serpent, but who cares, it was thrilling and frightening to us children in equal parts.

And then came the Suez Canal. The Canal itself was not especially spectacular, just a narrow channel of water with the desert on either side. One thing does, however, stand out in my mind and that is the indecent exposure of the Arabs which one would encounter along its reach. Upon seeing an approaching vessel they would position themselves at the top of the canal embankment, facing away from the ship, and then at the critical moment raise their *djelabahs*, and present their posteriors to the *ensemble* of passengers gathered on deck — this was in the years immediately following the Suez Crisis, it must be remembered. The more enterprising of their number even contrived to do their daily business whilst thus exposed and when anyone mentions the Suez Canal today, this is the image that first comes to mind: the golden glow of late afternoon sunlight on the desert sand, a blue and cloudless sky, white djelabahs fluttering in the breeze and a turd popping out of an Arab's backside.

After the Suez Canal, it was down the Red Sea to Aden. Blistering hot days with the desert heat from the arid lands on either side contributing to furnace-like temperatures that even the passage of the boat and sea breezes could not dispel. At this point in the voyage, the men would be allowed to discard their dinner jackets and adopt Red Sea Rig instead. The latter was a form of evening dress permissible in the sweaty latitudes of desert and jungle and consisted of black trousers worn with a white, short-sleeved shirt, cummerbund and black tie.

Aden, too, was hot, but I remember an evening drive in a hired car around the crater, the little white Arab houses built into the sloping walls like the troglodytes of Gaudiz. The lights were coming on all around the crater basin, twinkling in the still-shimmering air, while the jagged rim of the extinct volcano stood out sharply against the deepening indigo sky.

And then it was out into the Indian Ocean — the Erythrean Sea of the Ancients — a new world of monsoon seasons and tropical storms — we had reached Asia at last. "You can smell it in the air," my mother liked to say, and I would turn towards the Malabar Coast and inhale deeply, trying to catch the scent of the subcontinent, borne on the warm winds that blew across the Arabian Sea.

The Indian Ocean is vast and for days there would be nothing beyond the ship's rail for the eye to fix upon other than the serried ranks of wave crests and the occasional piece of passing flotsam. If lucky, we would, for a time, be escorted by a pod of dolphins who swam alongside our bows. Once we sailed through a sea of blood where a baby whale was being butchered by a school of sharks, but for the most part, it was just the ocean and plenty of it.

Then one day, out there on the horizon where the blue and boundless sky joined the blue and endless sea, there would be another ship! Great excitement! The Captain would come on the public address system and announce that "At approximately 3.20 this afternoon, we shall be passing the M.S. *Willem Ruys*," and we would fret away the intervening hours waiting for this tremendous event which was over almost before it began. The two ships would pass within fifty yards of each other to the accompaniment of blasts from their sirens and the tumultuous cheers of their passengers lining the rails. Some joker might blow a raspberry on a trumpet, much to everyone's amusement, but this cacophonous encounter lasted no more than a few brief instants — less time than it takes to read this paragraph — and then there would be just the sea and the sky again and a slightly different texture to the waves which marked the previous passage of our short-lived friends.

At each port of call, there would be a going-ashore party, which often entailed a visit to some local tourist attraction or place of special interest. On one occasion, I think it may have been at Karachi, we went to pay our respects to a sacred python that lived in a horrible dank cave, where incense and aromatic oils mingled noxiously with the smell of bat shit and urine. The venerated reptile inhabited a particularly pungent corner of this abominable place and there was an iron grille over the entrance to his lair. We peered dutifully for several minutes into this pit, but of the fabulous serpent we saw no sign.

If the ship put into Bombay, there would be an excursion to the Elephanta Caves, while Colombo meant a visit to the Mount Lavinia Hotel. The latter stood on a rocky peninsula, a few miles to the south of the city, and could be reached by rail, the train station being actually incorporated into the fabric of the hotel. It was a grand old place, the Ceylonese counterpart to Raffles, with gardens of hibiscus and frangipani, cooled by the ocean breezes, and a fine sandy beach at the bottom of the cliffs where one could swim.

After leaving Colombo, one sailed for Penang and though crossing the Bay of Bengal only took a matter of days, I remember that on one occasion, it was this part of the voyage when scurvy broke out among the children on board — we were passengers on a cargo vessel and the galley had run out of fresh fruit and green vegetables. Huge pustular boils erupted on my forehead and neck, which had to be lanced by the ship's medical officer. On arrival at George Town, the mothers of the children on board sallied forth on the first boat to shore in a quest for vitamin C — lots of it. They returned with dozens of little jars of Heinz' *purée* of spinach, which was spooned into us like corn into a *foie gras* goose. Although the beastly stuff looked and smelt like duck shit, it was certainly efficacious and within a couple of days the boils and lesions had all but disappeared.

My father would usually leave the ship at Penang and take the overnight train from Butterworth to Singapore in order to hasten his return to work, but my mother and I would remain on board to complete the last leg of our voyage, down the Malacca Straits. A couple of days later and we would be steaming into Keppel Harbour where biscuit-coloured tugboats, with funnels belching black smoke, would take our hawser and gently manoeuvre us into our berth — the six-week, nine-thousand-mile voyage was over.

Inevitably, there would be a party of friends waiting on the quayside to welcome us. At a time when 'Home leave' only came around once every two and a half years and was of six months' duration, departures and returns were sufficient cause for much celebration and going down to the docks at Tanjong Pagar to 'meet the boat' or 'see people off' was an enthusiastically-embraced pastime.

Departures tended to be the more prolonged and exuberant affairs as everyone got caught up in the excitement of the moment. Six month's leave! One hundred and eighty days! One could really do something with that amount of time: rent a house, write a book, get married (many did) — anything was possible. Down at the docks it was like Christmas day, with paper streamers fluttering down from the decks and a musical accompaniment provided by the ship's dance band. Everyone's health was toasted a dozen times over and then again for good measure.

"Look at those young men," my mother said, "they seem to be having a good time." It is four o'clock in the afternoon and the sun shines warmly down on the quayside where four young Englishmen in their shirt sleeves, their collars loosened, their neckties at half mast, are stumbling along, a little red in the face, though not from the sun, their arms around each other's shoulders, laughing good-naturedly and bellowing their farewells to a departing colleague who leans over the ship's rails high above us. I never saw any of them again, but to this day, whenever I hear the expression 'young man,' it is always those four friends, a little rowdy and inebriated, but not in an unpleasant way, who come to mind, though they must be well into their sixties by now, if they haven't already succumbed to the demon drink.

But all of this was many years ago and the leisurely days of passenger liners and voyages by sea are long gone. After all, who today could set aside six whole weeks of their life just to get from Singapore to London? Indeed, in an age when one can telephone one's office from an aeroplane at 30,000 feet over the Hindu Kush, to travel anywhere by ship seems an almost indecent dereliction of duty. No, I don't suppose that many of us will go down to the sea in ships again, unless it be for some blanket-wrapped, nonagenarian winter cruise in the Aegean. And more's the pity, I think, for an SQ 747 Megatop is no substitute for a slow boat to China and no airline dinner, not even in First Class, could ever match the *smörgåsbord* splendours of a Danish sea captain's table.

THOSE BLUE REMEMBERED HILLS

At the top of the watershed a government resthouse serves as a shelter for travellers ...
A resplendent table had been prepared; all the government crockery and silver with the
bull's head crest, the whole stock of bottles arrayed like skittles on the sideboard. There
had been a massacre in the fowl-run, and the kitchen garden swept bare; cocks, ducks,
a sucking pig were laid before us, and European vegetables which the cook had grown,
and six green strawberries — his pride. He applied to us for an increase of wages ... But
best and most unlooked-for of welcomes — tall flames were dancing in a fireplace.

— Henri Fauconnier, *The Soul of Malaya* (1931) —

There was a time when I thought that the most desirable place to live in all the world would be at the top of Fraser's Hill, a modest peak in the range of mountains that runs down the spine of the Malay Peninsula. It was a most salubrious and invigorating location. In the dry months, the climate was like a perfect summer's day in England, while in the rainy season, well, it was like a typical summer's day in England.

Fraser's Hill was what was known as a 'hill station,' a legacy of the colonial era when Englishmen and their families would periodically retire to the mountains for a spot of 'local leave.' At a time when it was only possible to return to England once every three or four years, the hills were where one went for rest and recreation. After the tropic heat of the lowlands, the cooler climes at higher altitudes and the frequent Scotch mists that rolled down from the surrounding peaks, reminded the expatriate of autumnal days back 'Home,' an impression made all the more vivid by the ritual lighting of a log fire in the evenings, despite the fact that the ambient temperature seldom dropped below 65° Fahrenheit.

Fraser's Hill, and all the other places like it in Malaya — Penang Hill, Maxwell Hill and the Cameron Highlands — had their origins in India, in the great hill stations of Simla, Darjeeling and Ootacamund. At the outset, they were envisaged primarily as sanitaria, a place for tired Company men, debilitated by dysentery, malaria, swamp fever and other tropical malaises. One therefore finds that every hill station has a bungalow named 'Convalescent' reflecting these early beginnings. Subsequently, they evolved into the Eastern equivalent of a spa town and like Cheltenham and Harrogate, or for that matter the great spa resorts of Switzerland, they became as much associated with leisure and amusement as with the restoration of health and vigour.

Each hill station had its own particular atmosphere and charm. Penang Hill, the oldest in Malaya, floated above George Town on a pillow of orthographic cloud, suspended in the ether like an *hashshshin* dream of Paradise. Surrounded by jungle, it could only be reached by funicular railway, or on foot, though my grandmother once made the ascent in a palanquin. The view from the summit is magnificent — a panoramic vista of George Town and the narrow straits separating Penang island from the mainland, with Kedah peak in the distance. James Brooke, who was later to become the first 'White Rajah' of Sarawak, described the scene as a "landscape of vast extent, and so diversified that the eye never wearies of gazing." And the microclimate at the top was no less stimulating: John Turnbull Thomson, Singapore's first town planner, enthused that the air on the "Great Hill [was] buoyant, cool, elevating to the spirits, bracing to the nerves and exciting to the appetite."

Long ago, there was a famous hotel at the top of Penang Hill, called the Crag, which was run by the Sarkies brothers of Raffles fame — they also owned the splendid 'E & O' (Eastern & Oriental) Hotel down below in George Town. According to my grandmother, the place was haunted: one would awake at night to hear the sound of a woman in bustle skirts rushing along the corridor, her dress brushing against the wall and her breath coming in short gasps like someone who had been running hard or was in distress.

Even today, Penang Hill still retains the magical charm that is so beguilingly captured in William Daniell's aquatints from the early years of the nineteenth century. Hilltop bungalows, surrounded by jungle-clad slopes, and majestic views with picturesque cloud formations, Daniell's Penang prints were the Malayan equivalent of the fox-hunting, grouse-shooting, fly-fishing genre of sporting prints that gentrified the walls of countless middle-class homes back in England.

The Cameron Highlands, in the state of Perak, were more like Scotland, with its bracken-bordered golf course and pine trees, and one could readily imagine a lone stag silhouetted, Landseer-like, against the lowering skies. It was also strongly reminiscent of that other piece of errant Caledonia, misplaced upon a tropical mountaintop, Nuwara Eliya, in Ceylon, with its attendant tea plantations and lake. This last impression was reinforced by the presence of a large population of Indian tea pickers who worked for the local Boh Tea company, which had extensive estates in the Cameron Highlands. Every so often, I recall, a tea picker would get carried off by a tiger, which used to cause a bit of a stir.

By far the nicest place to stay in the Cameron Highlands was at the old Smoke House, an extraordinary architectural confabulation of half-timbered, stockbroker Tudor, with tall Elizabethan brick chimneys and rough-plastered walls. There were leaded lights in the windows and roses round the door, and the place looked for all the world like a rather agreeable country hotel in England — the King's Head, it would have been called, or the County Arms. The illusion continued indoors, where one stepped into a world of exposed beams, ingle nooks and polished horse brass. The breakfast room was all chintz and floral wallpaper; the snug bar a solid piece of *meranti* with the beer on tap, though it was only the same old Anchor that frothed from the spout. Copper bed-warming pans hung from the walls and a fire blazed in the grate at night. Yes, it might well have been the Home Counties, were it not for the riot of tropical vegetation at the end of the garden and the fact that tiger pug marks were occasionally found on the lawn in the mornings.

Of all the hill stations, however, Fraser's Hill was my favourite. It was at once an English village and a frontier town, a miniature Darjeeling as far removed from everyday life in Kuala Lumpur as the foothills of the Himalayas. There was a pub — the Tavern it was called — a post office, a general store and a dispensary, and these formed the nucleus of the community. There was also a dairy farm and a flower nursery, which provided roses and chrysanthemums for the hotels and florists of Kuala Lumpur. And there were a couple of dozen bungalows built of stone and timber, half-hidden amongst the Scotch pines or placed on little eminences that overlooked the modest nine-hole golf course around which this strange tableau of idealised village England was set. Again, it could have been Surrey, were it not for a dramatic backdrop of jungle-clad mountains, with deep, mist-filled valleys that echoed to a dawn chorus of gibbons.

Fraser's Hill was called after a muleteer by the name of Louis James Fraser who ran a transportation service between Kuala Kubu Bahru and Raub. This was in the last years of the nineteenth century when a proper road linking the East and West Coasts had yet to be cut through the central mountain range that divides the Malay Peninsula longitudinally in two. Fraser built himself a bungalow halfway along the trail, so that he could break the journey in two and in so doing gave his name to the peak that rose behind his house. Someone who knew Fraser in later life described him as "a frail old man [who] had some disfigurement to one eye." But Fraser was a lot tougher than he looked. On one occasion, his Malay servants, thinking he had died, had actually started to bury him when suddenly the 'corpse' came to life and called an immediate halt to the proceedings.

Fraser eventually did die, some time in the early 1900s, and soon afterwards a trunk road was carved through the mountains linking Selangor and Pahang. A government resthouse was built at the highest point, where the road crosses over the watershed and passes from one state into the other. This narrow corridor through the mountains is called, appropriately enough, 'the Gap', and judging from photographs the winding road that leads up there from Kuala Kubu Bahru, looks pretty much the same today as it did in the early years of the last century.

Kuala Kubu Bahru, or KKB as it was known in the argot of the old Malaya hand, was, and still is, a delightful place, exemplifying the sort of small provincial town that was once a characteristic feature of Peninsular Malaya not so many years ago, but which sadly have all but disappeared in the past quarter of a century. It stands at the foot of the mountains, neat and tidy, with a freshly-scrubbed look about it. There is a police station and a post office, a few broad streets of shophouses with awnings shading their five-foot ways, and some nicely-laid-out ornamental gardens. One can actually get there by train from Kuala Lumpur, though the station is a few miles down the road on the mainline between KL and Ipoh. Interestingly, the railway station at Kuala Kubu Road is where the original Kuala Kubu was situated — the latter disappeared under a slough of silt washed down from nearby tin mines.

There is also a large military garrison stationed at Kuala Kubu Bahru, a legacy of the Malayan Emergency, when the British Army was engaged in an undeclared war against Communist insurgents in the jungles of Malaysia. Back then — the Emergency lasted from 1948 until 1960 — KKB stood in the middle of 'bandit country', the forest-clad slopes of the surrounding hills with their hidden valleys and secret trails providing the perfect hideaway for 'CTs' as the Communist terrorists were usually known. The latter were for the most part extremely dedicated men and women, many of whom had been living in the jungle since the Second World War, their commitment to their cause fuelled by a Utopian vision of a New Malaya, freed not only of the colonial yoke (or whatever the Chinese equivalent of the hackneyed phrase is), but also from all other forms of social inequality and injustice. The story is well told in Noel Barber's *The War of the Running Dogs*, and a good story it is too, though with many a sad and savage moment. There is also a sympathetic, insider's account of life in a forest hideaway in Spencer Chapman's *The Jungle is Neutral*, which tells of his wartime experiences in occupied Malaya, when he found refuge, first with the Orang Asli, and then later with the Communists who in those days shared a common enemy with the British.

When I was a child, although the Emergency had been officially declared over, there were still a fair number of CTs holed up in the jungle, and military checkpoints continued to be posted along the highways and byways of the Malay Peninsula, which made a journey to the mountains seem all the more exciting for a small boy.

Kuala Kubu Bahru nestles at the very foot of the mountains which divide the Peninsula in two and the ascent to Fraser's Hill began immediately the town was left behind on the road heading east towards Pahang. Quite soon one came to a Bailey bridge spanning a narrow gorge with a fast-flowing river at the bottom, strewn with rocks and huge boulders. There were further glimpses of this mountain-fed torrent for the next couple of miles along the road and if one stopped the car to admire the view, its rushing waters could be heard turning over the stones in the river bed in their impatience to get to the sea. It was a wonderful river in those days, but the last time I passed that way it ran slow and sluggish and its once crystal-clear waters are now the colour of coffee shop tea — that is to say, bright orange. The signs were all too familiar. Logging and deforestation further upstream have allowed the monsoon rains to wash away a forest floor that was a million years deep in humus, exposing the red, raw, worthless laterite soils beneath, and these in turn have ended up in the once-pristine river, clogging its arteries with a thick, sclerotic sediment that has choked the life from its now oxygen-depleted waters.

But all this lay in the future and it never occurred to me then that this beautiful country, with its jungles and tigers and wild places that literally lay within sight of the main road, could all but disappear within twenty-five years. It was here that my mother saw a *seladang* — a massive wild ox (*Bos gaurus*), standing tall as a man at the shoulder. It was just by the roadside, silent and unmoving, a rare sighting, even in those days, but there again my mother has seen many marvellous things, including a *yeti* in Kashmir (though it might have been a bear).

Which reminds me, there was a family friend who once saw a very curious creature along the same stretch of road. It was early one morning and the sun had already risen, but the day was still young, and Bernard was on his way down from Fraser's Hill after spending the weekend there with his family. The latter were staying on at 'Fraser's' for a few extra days and Bernard was alone, driving unhurriedly along, when his attention was suddenly caught by the sight of a strange animal standing upright on a dead branch, a hundred yards or so from the road. He stopped the car for a better look and was able to note that the creature, which was covered in thick dark hair, was anthropoid in form, but very much larger than a *siamang* (gibbon). Moreover, its posture was erect, rather than stooped, as if bipedal locomotion were its normal gait. Bernard looked at the creature and the creature looked at Bernard. And after a few minutes Bernard got back in the car and went on his way, very much regretting the fact that he'd left his binoculars with his family.

Now Bernard was a straightforward, no-nonsense Yorkshireman, and though he might occasionally have liked a drink or two, this was a bright and sunny morning and he was on his way to work after a relaxing weekend in the mountains. Nor was he the sort of person to spin a yarn. Indeed, he was, for the most part, a fairly taciturn sort of fellow who only told my mother about the sighting because he knew that she was 'interested' is such things.

So what exactly did Bernard see? There are no *orang utan* outside of zoos in the Malay Peninsula, and anyway the animal was more hominid than simian. As it happens, in those days, alleged sightings of this mysterious creature were quite common. Indeed, one often read about them in the newspaper — an Indian rubber tapper making his morning rounds would catch sight of a strange figure, like a man but unclothed and extremely hairy, flitting through the shadows in the half-light of early dawn. Sometimes, it was a couple, the female with an infant at her breast, but always they slipped silently away into the forest, half-real, half-imagined, watching from just beyond the margins of civilisation, an alter ego that may have been entirely chimerical, or maybe not.

Sadly, it is hard to believe in such encounters nowadays. These sort of stories can't really exist in modern Malaysia — barrelling along the north-south highway, cocooned in air-conditioned comfort, with the radio on, one cannot really entertain the thought of some shy denizen of the forest depths, half-man, half-ape, gazing out at one from the trees. But not so very long ago, it seemed quite plausible that such creatures might exist — the Orang Asli knew all about them — and as a child, I would scan the dense vegetation at the side of the road in the hope of catching a glimpse of these strange forest folk.

But to return to the road up to Fraser's Hill, as soon as it left the river, it began to twist and turn back on itself as the ascent commenced in earnest. Its edge was marked by white-painted stones and it followed the contours of the mountain, with a steep mossy bank on one side and an all-but-precipitous drop on the other. Here and there one had an impression of distant vistas, glimpsed through a screen of huge dipterocarp trees, with massive trunks, that rose, straight as a plumb line from the forest floor, soaring eighty feet or more before branching into a crown of verdant foliage. There were also stands of giant bamboos, which could grow a foot overnight, their culms as thick as telegraph poles. And just occasionally, one would pass a tree in flower, a splash of orange or vermilion blossom against a backdrop of variegated sage and olive greens.

The air was pierced by the 'zing' of cicadas and from every direction came the tinkling sound of running water, splashing into pools and tumbling over little cascades, no doubt destined for the racing river now left far below. The road wound on and upwards, doubling back on itself every two hundred yards or so in a dizzying succession of steeply-cambered hairpin bends. At two thousand feet one came to the first tree ferns, with their delicate tracery and diamond-pattern trunks — they are among the most ancient of living plant forms with a lineage stretching back to the primeval forests of the Carboniferous Period some three hundred million years ago.

Just before arriving at the Gap, one came to the spot where Sir Henry Gurney was ambushed and killed by CTs in October 1951. It was a completely freak incident and it was only later that those who took part in the attack were aware of the devastating blow they had struck — that in one swift burst of machine-gun fire they had succeeded in wiping out the plenipotentiary of imperial might in Malaya, none other than the British High Commissioner himself. It was easy to imagine the scene: thirty seconds' automatic fire from the trees and then a stunned silence, the cicadas hushed; the black staff car stationary in the middle of the road, the Union Jack on its bonnet hanging limp; the drip of petrol escaping from a punctured fuel tank and the murmur of cooling water in the radiator; the doors flung open and the body of Sir Henry lying on the road — he had got out of the car to draw the fire away from his wife and was killed almost instantly in a hail of bullets. The air seemed colder here and there was a little Chinese shrine placed at the foot of a large tree by the edge of the road, perhaps intended to appease the raging spirits of the angry dead.

Another couple of bends in the road and one came to the Gap. There was a little police station here — a wooden bungalow affair, neatly painted blue and white, with a row of fire buckets hanging from the eaves and a bed of golden marigolds in front. Directly opposite, stood a Chinese eatery — a rickety shack perched precariously at the very edge of the road where the mountainside plunged away steeply into dense foliage. It served cold drinks and the usual *mah-mee* fare to long-distance truck drivers hungry for calories after hauling their cumbersome vehicles round the serpentine mountain bends that stretched from Kuala Kubu Bahru to the top of the pass.

The Gap resthouse stands above the road at the top of a high embankment with a stone retaining wall. It is a solid building, set foursquare, with thick granite walls and quoins at the corners — a chunk of Scottish baronial, built to withstand cold winters and the assault of border reivers, the nostalgic creation of some homesick Scotsman, pining in the Public Works Department.

This was the place to stop for a cold beer after the drive up from Kuala Lumpur. Even though the altitude at the Gap is only a little over 2,000 feet — barely half the height of Fraser's Hill — one could already discern a perceptible change in the climate. The air was much cooler and fresher here, and there were roses and nasturtiums, pansies and petunias, not forgetting the ubiquitous marigold, growing in the flowerbeds of the neatly-tended resthouse gardens.

The 'English' flowers were a delight, but they were no match for the forest which rose up the mountainsides in every direction, an unbroken canopy of green, pierced by the occasional dead tree, its bleached trunk and denuded branches starkly white against the surrounding foliage. One almost always saw hornbills at the Gap and they were usually to be spotted on one of these dead trees, attracting attention to themselves by their raucous honking. When they took to the air, their flight was truly awe-inspiring, the great 'whoosh' from the downdraft of their enormous wings, carrying across the valleys like the slow chuffing of a steam locomotive.

To make the final ascent to Fraser's Hill itself, one left the trunk road at the Gap and the incline was so steep in places and the road so narrow, that motor traffic was restricted to going in one direction at a time — odd hours up and even hours down. In these last five miles the altitude was doubled and the vegetation changed again; now one had unbroken views across the vastness of the rain forest, which in those days seemed to be without end, the terrain rising and falling in a succession of ridges, peaks and valleys that formed the corrugated backbone of the Malay Peninsula. Then suddenly, one was at the top and had entered another world where all the dogs had a corkscrew twist in their tails and the natives wore cardigans and knitted tam-o'-shanters.

Most of the houses at Fraser's Hill were built in the 1920s and '30s and the architecture tended towards the slightly fantastic — Anglo-Indian bungalows with verandahs, dressed up in the clothes of *cottage orné*, augmented by various Arts and Crafts stylings, with a dash of Voysey thrown in for good measure. They had tiled roofs and granite walls, and inside the wooden floors were spread with rather threadbare *kilims*. And of course, every house came with at least one open fireplace — lighting a fire in the evenings was a keenly-anticipated feature of the holidays, at once a reminder of 'Home' and also something far deeper — the Promethian memories of an ancient Palaeolithic past that stir in the breast of any fire-gazer.

These magical pavilions were set in jewel-like gardens, with neatly-mown lawns and morning glory rampaging over everything. In this perpetual summertime, the roses were always in bloom and a wide variety of temperate species flourished — hydrangeas, gardenias, gladioli, irises, sweet peas — anything, it seemed, could grow in that salubrious air. Naturally, every house had its own vegetable plot which produced a limitless supply of broad beans, *mange tout*, baby carrots, and new potatoes, not to mention strawberries all the year round. These gardens were tended by the resident cookboy and his *amah* wife who together looked after the running of the bungalow, making sure there were clean sheets on the beds and wood for the fire.

So what did one do? Well there were over thirty miles of jungle pathways and trails requiring varying degrees of fitness and vigour, and 'going for a walk' was probably the number one pastime for all but the least energetically inclined. But there was also a modest nine-hole golf and tennis courts for the sporting types and bird watching and butterfly collecting for those whose interests lay elsewhere. Fraser's Hill abounded in winged life forms and those who enjoyed skewering lepidopterons on the end of a pin had a field day. All that was necessary was to sprinkle a bit of salt on a sunny rock and then wait a short while — within five minutes there would be a cloud of fabulously-coloured butterflies flitting about the salt deposit on iridescent wings. I preferred that they should stay that way, and I didn't care much for the collectors with their nets and snuff bottles.

Speaking of insects reminds me that down at the dispensary there was a singular collection of bugs and other interesting creatures — snakes, toads, two-head foetuses and the like — preserved in alcohol in large glass jars. There were huge cicadas, and scorpions, and centipedes eighteen inches long, not to mention the enormous hairy tarantulas and stick insects as big as coat-hangers. Fraser's Hill seemed to encourage an isolated form of giganticism in its insect population and one trembled to think what might be lurking in a leafy bed of nasturtiums.

Food was a big thing too. The cool mountain air and outdoor activities stimulated gargantuan appetites that could only be satisfied by hearty English breakfasts, a substantial lunch, afternoon tea with several rounds of sandwiches and a hefty slice of fruit cake, and finally, a three-course dinner in the evening. The cookboys at Fraser's Hill seemed to have been universally educated in the Anglo-Indian school of colonial cuisine, and to a man served up great plates of scrambled eggs and kedgeree for breakfast, tureens of mulligatawny soup for lunch, and fish Mornay followed by a side of beef for dinner, with new potatoes and velvety broad beans, fresh from the garden. And then there was the ubiquitous crème caramel for desert — no meal, it seemed, could be brought to a proper conclusion without one of these slippery, quaking custards.

After dinner there were books to be read and playing cards and board games and whiskey for the grown ups and fireside reveries. The appreciable drop in temperature at night, especially when it rained, seemed like a cold front passing by and it was enough just to sit beside the fire and toss orange peel and pine cones into the flames, filling the room with their fragrance. And then one went to bed — the combined effect of vigorous exercise, repletion and a log fire usually meant that this was at a fairly early hour. As one's feet touched the cold and, it must be said, often damp sheets, thoughts of boarding school and freezing dormitories came fleetingly to mind, but that only made it seem twice as good to be where one was, knowing that in the morning one would awaken to a dawn chorus of chortling tropic birdsong and the crow of the cookboy's rooster, not the tolling of a hand bell and the prospect of congealed porridge for breakfast.

Ultimately a large part of the charm of Fraser's Hill, and the other hill stations like it, lay in the meeting of opposites — an English village set down in the jungle, an outpost of civilisation in the midst of a wilderness. But there was also a reflexive quality, which fed upon a Romantic past that was linked to India and the recently-dismantled Raj — I am thinking back some thirty-five years ago. This was a world that drew breath from Kipling's *Plain Tales from the Hills*, but which even then was already being reconstituted by the likes of Paul Scott and M. M. Kaye as part of a burgeoning nostalgia for a quasi-mythical British India of *nabobs, memsahibs* and *maharajahs*. In this last respect, Fraser's Hill was rather like an Eastern Portmeirion, an elaborate fantasy where nothing was quite what it seemed. One could easily have imagined oneself to be in England as one sipped one's pint beside the fire in the Tavern, or challenged someone to a game of bar-billiards. Yet one knew that just beyond those shuttered windows lay an enormous tract of virgin rainforest, stretching all the way to the Thai border and beyond, a wild and mountainous realm where the tiger still roamed and Orang Asli huntsmen stalked their prey with blowpipes. And there was also the thought that somewhere out there, in some lost valley obscured by the clouds, one might yet find that strange creature, neither fully man nor wholly beast, a missing link in the chain of human evolution, peering out from a darkened cave mouth or standing silently beside a jungle stream.

Along the smooth and slender wires, the sleepless heralds run,
Fast as the clear and living rays go streaming from the sun;
No pearls of flashes, heard or seen, their wondrous flight betray,
And yet their words are quickly caught in cities far away.

—An anonymous Pennsylvania preacher (1848) —

❖

Inevitably one hears an awful lot about the revolutionary times in which we live, the revolution in this instance being brought about not by guns and grenades but by the gentle tip-tapping of a keyboard and the silent, electrical synapses inside my computer. Scarcely a week goes by without there being some programme on the BBC extolling the virtues of an information superhighway and excitedly enthusing about the marvellous benefits that even greater globalisation will bring. I will pass over my scepticism about the latter, for the time being, while as far as enjoyment is concerned, I'd much rather listen to the radio than surf the Internet any day. The Internet is tiresome with its comic-strip graphics and its exhortations to buy this, sell that, get up close with Fann Wong or collect telephone cards with pictures of Mickey Mouse on them. The wireless on the other hand is like chatting to a good friend, except that the friend does all the talking; it has a conversational intimacy that is completely lacking in television and which the Internet can never hope to achieve.

And just how revolutionary is the Internet anyway? To begin with, given the fact that some 80 percent of the world's population doesn't have access to a telephone, let alone a computer, this is a revolution that is going to pass a lot of people by. Secondly, as far as the speedy transmission of breaking news is concerned, I'm not convinced that the Internet is any faster than the wireless. As for the quality of information conveyed via the net, it seems to me that an awful lot of the traffic proceeding along the information superhighway is carrying a pretty banal or commonplace load. What is more, the interstices of much of the world-wide web are so clogged with the goo of pop-trivia and other forms of pulp faction that more often than not, I quit the net without having found what I was looking for. The occasional lucky strike aside, if I had the *Encyclopaedia Britannica* on my bookshelves, I wouldn't even bother to log on. And I haven't yet mentioned the prodigious quantities of pornography that thrusts its way, unsolicited, onto my monitor screen — a recent search for information on Gunong Tahan, the highest mountain in Peninsular Malaysia, led me directly to the home page of 'Malaysian Girls Looking for Sex' (since deleted). All of which is not to say that there aren't some excellent websites and interesting forums for debate on the Internet, but equally there is a huge amount of misinformation floating around out there in the æther of cyberspace. In more cynical moments it occurs to me that the Internet is rather like a chorus of Chinese whispers, vicariously feeding on one another and all the while increasing exponentially in volume, like a strand of mutant RNA running wild in a bowl of amino acids. If ever the medium was the message, then surely it was the Internet.

But to get back to the idea of a communications revolution, to my mind the advent of cable telegraphy was far more revolutionary in terms of the impact it made on the global exchange of information than either the invention of wireless telegraphy which followed some time afterwards, or the satellite and glass-fibre technologies of today. In the last quarter of the nineteenth century, for example, news from London could reach Singapore by telegraph in a matter of hours and be published in the *Singapore Chronicle* the very next day. Now *that* was revolutionary compared with the situation that had existed before the advent of telegraphy, when it had taken some four to five weeks for the European news to get here. And that was *after* the introduction of steam navigation and the opening of the Suez Canal in 1859, which preceded the cable connection by some ten years; in the days of sail and rounding the Cape, communication with England of course took far longer.

In an instant, then, cable telegraphy completely transformed the nature of global communications. Nothing would ever be quite the same again. Not even bouncing messages off satellites in orbit around the earth has represented such a dramatic advance in the way we transmit news and information, worldwide, as that first, telegraphic revolution.

*

Charles Wheatstone, together with his partner, William Fothergill Cooke, are generally credited as being the inventors of modern electrical telegraphy, though a letter to the *Scots' Magazine*, published on 17th February 1753, entitled *An expeditious method for conveying intelligence*, reveals that in principle, at least, electrical telegraphy was already known in the mid-eighteenth century. Wheatstone was originally a musical instrument maker and his interest in sound led him, in the 1830s, to experiment with electrical communication. He became Professor of Experimental Philosophy at Kings College London and was elected a Fellow of the Royal Society in 1836. The following year, he was introduced to William Fothergill Cooke, who was also working along similar lines, and they joined forces to develop a viable system of electrical telegraphy. This was first demonstrated to the public on 24th July 1837, when they ran a telegraph line along the railway track from Euston to Camden Town and successfully transmitted and received a message.

At almost exactly the same time that Wheatstone and Cooke were demonstrating their new invention in England, Samuel Morse was conducting a similar experiment in the United States. In terms of historical precedent, the Englishmen had the slight edge on their American rival. The first patent for Wheatstone and Cooke's "five-needle" telegraph — described as a "Method of Giving Signals and Sounding Alarums at Distant Places by Means of Electric Currents Transmitted through Metallic Circuits" — was registered on 12th June 1837, while the first demonstration of Morse's "pendulum" telegraph took place at New York University on 3rd September of that year.

Morse immediately presented his new invention to the United States Congress to be considered as a means of communication between New York and New Orleans, but his proposal was rejected and it was several more years before Morse could finally convince the authorities of the usefulness of his device: the famous first message — "What hath God wrought?" — sent by Morse to inaugurate the first American electrical telegraph line from Washington to Baltimore, dates from 24th May 1844.

That was the turning point, though, and within a matter of years electrical telegraphy had successfully routed its optical predecessor, on land, if not at sea. By 1851, even the Stock Exchanges in London and Paris were connected by cable. There was still, however, one final barrier that had to be overcome before electrical telegraphy could be said to have revolutionised global communications and that was the oceans.

In the early days of landline telegraphy, the oceans presented an insuperable obstacle to telegraphic communications between the continents. Despite the existence of a burgeoning network of landlines, when it came to crossing the Atlantic, messages between Europe and America still had to be conveyed by ship. One of the problems was that before telegraph cables could work under water, it was necessary to develop a cable with good waterproofing and electrical insulation. Interestingly, one of the technological breakthroughs that helped establish the submarine cable in favour of landlines came from this part of the world — I refer here to the development of gutta-percha as an insulating material. Gutta-percha is the milky, latex-like resin of various Malaysian trees of the sapodilla family, especially *Palaquium gutta* (the term 'gutta' is a corruption of the Malay word *getah* meaning 'sap' or 'resin'). Locally-made items of gutta-percha were brought to Europe from the Malay Peninsula and were exhibited at the Royal Society of Arts in London in 1843. In a pre-polymer world, the plastic qualities of gutta-percha seemed rather marvellous and it was soon being put to a variety of uses, including jewellery-making, dentistry and the manufacture of golf balls. Then, in 1845, S. W. Silver & Co. of Stratford, East London, invented a means of extruding gutta-percha to cover wire which enabled it to be used as an insulting material for marine cables and other electrical devices — the problem of waterproofing was solved.

There was, however, a second difficulty faced by the manufacturers of intercontinental submarine cables and telegraph cables generally, and this was the ability to generate a strong enough current to travel along a thousand or more miles of wire. Landline telegraph lines at this time were only a few hundred miles in length: to transmit a message any further required manual or electromechanical relay of the message. Obviously this was not possible in the case of submarine cables between the continents, which meant that the current at the far end of a cable was very weak indeed — there was simply not enough charge in the system to pull the electromagnets of a telegraph sounder.

This lead to the invention of what was called a mirror galvanometer which was employed at the receiving end of a telegraphic transmission. Galvanometers are very sensitive devices and will respond to even the weakest currents. In the case of the mirror galvanometer, the attachment of a mirror with a light source placed in front of it enabled a telegraph operator, sitting in a darkened room, to register any movement of the galvanometer simply by watching the light projected by the mirror on a wall or a scale positioned a few feet away. At the transmitting end, two keys connected to electrical poles were used to make the dots and dashes. Depressing one key, sent a positive voltage along the wire, while pushing the other sent a negative charge — the effect at the other end was to cause the galvanometer to swing either to the left or to the right, representing a dot or a dash accordingly.

All this was pretty Heath-Robinson and there were several disadvantages. In the first place, it took two men to operate the system — one to watch the beam of light and call out the letters and another to write them down. Secondly, there was no permanent record of the message received other than the scribbled transcription. These limitations were eventually overcome by the invention of the 'siphon recorder' in 1873 by none other than Lord Kelvin (then plain William Thomson) of absolute zero fame. This device worked by passing a siphon of ink transversely back and forth across a thin paper tape which was itself in motion, the principle here being rather like that of a drum barograph. The movement of the ink jet was effected by the flow of an electrical current through a coil to which the siphon was mechanically attached, thereby enabling the message to be permanently transcribed on the tickertape.

The first submarine cable linking Europe and North America was laid between Newfoundland and Valentia, Ireland, in 1858. The world marvelled, Queen Victoria and the US President, James Buchanan, exchanged messages, and someone by the name of Francis H. Brown composed a piece of music entitled 'The Ocean Telegraph March.' Unfortunately, the cable was only in service twenty-three days before it failed and it was not until after the end of the American Civil War that another attempt was made. In 1865 a second cable broke while being laid in deep water, but in 1866 a third cable was successfully deployed and a permanent telegraphic link between Europe and the Americas was established.

Described by Arthur C. Clarke as the Victorian equivalent of the Apollo project, the laying of the Atlantic telegraph cable was largely masterminded by one man, John Pender, an ambitious entrepreneur whose prescience ultimately led to the formation of the world's first and largest global communications network, Cable and Wireless. Born in Scotland, in 1815, Pender left school to work in a local factory which produced cotton and textiles. He was managing director at the age of twenty-one and by the time he was twenty-five he had moved to Glasgow and set himself up as a cotton merchant. He later relocated to Manchester where he formed John Pender & Company, which became a leading distributor of cotton products from Lancashire and Scotland. A well-known figure at the Manchester Cotton Exchange, Pender subsequently invested his money in the Anglo-Irish Magnetic Telegraph Company. This was in 1852 and was the first step to his becoming a major player in the world of nineteenth-century international communications.

In 1856, John Pender became a director of the Atlantic Telegraph Company and in 1864 he formed the cable-manufacturing company Telcon (Telegraph Construction and Maintenance Company) with an immediate commission to supply £700,000 worth of submarine telegraph cable to span the Atlantic Ocean. An agreement was simultaneously reached with the Great Eastern Steamship Company to deploy their huge ocean liner, the *Great Eastern*, as a cableship. Being five times larger than any vessel previously built — she displaced some 18,000 tons and was 700 feet in length — the *Great Eastern* was the only ship large enough, at that time, to carry the single length of cable needed to span the Atlantic Ocean.

With the technology and the physical means now in place, the following year, John Pender co-founded the Anglo-American Telegraph Company to lay the new Atlantic cable. The cable itself, manufactured by Pender's cable-making company, Telcon, was both lighter and stronger than the previous cables which had failed, and on the morning of 27th July 1866, the *Great Eastern* hove to off the shores of Newfoundland with the live end of the transatlantic link on board. By noon the same day, the cable had been successfully landed at the settlement of Heart's Content and the oceanic divide was no more.

Once the all-important connection between Europe and America had been achieved, John Pender was quick to turn his thoughts to the British Empire, with India at the top of his list. Up until 1870, telegraph communications between the subcontinent and Europe were provided by the Turkish State landlines which ran from Constantinople (Istanbul) to Fao in the Persian Gulf via Baghdad. In 1868, however, the Indo-European Telegraph Company was formed in Germany to provide a speedier and more reliable means of communication between England and India. This was achieved in 1870, when the company completed a line from England to Teheran (via Germany and South Russia), where it joined the Indian Government landline to Bushehr and then on to Karachi and the subcontinent.

In the same year, though, the first submarine cable link to India was completed by John Pender's British Indian Submarine Telegraph Company. The latter stretched all the way from Porthcurno, in Cornwall, to Bombay, taking in Portugal, Gibraltar, Malta, Alexandria and Aden along the way. Although in itself a remarkable achievement, this was just the first step in

Pender's ambitious plan to provide a cable service that would encircle the globe. Even before the link between Britain and India was completed, John Pender had already formed the China Submarine Telegraph Company to lay a 1,700-mile cable between Singapore and Shanghai, via Saigon and Hong Kong. That was in December 1869, and the following year he set up the British Australian Telegraph Company to connect Singapore with Port Darwin in the Northern Territory. By the end of 1871, an undersea cable linking Singapore and Penang with Madras was in place, and with the completion of the Chinese and Australian connections, Singapore became the epicentre of a huge regional communications network that joined Australasia and the Far East to Europe and the USA.

Other extensions followed and by the time of Pender's death in 1896, at the age of eighty, even the most far-flung islands of the Indian Ocean had been linked to the first world-wide web. Not only had Pender's vision of a global telegraph service been realised, but it had effectively become the central nervous system of the British Empire. Knighted in 1888, Sir John's name is commemorated here in Singapore by Pender Road, which winds up the western flank of Mount Faber — the black and white bungalows halfway up the hill were built in the 1920s for senior staff members of what had by then become the Eastern Extension, Australasia & China Telegraph Company, later to be reconstituted as Cable and Wireless.

And here I have to declare a personal interest in this history of the first global communications revolution, for my maternal grandfather was one of those who manned what was perhaps the most remote cable station in the entire network, the island of Rodriguez, a tiny speck, half the size of Singapore, in the vastness of the Indian Ocean. I never knew him personally for he was dead long before I was born, but I remember in my grandmother's house in Coulsdon, in a glass-fronted cabinet in the entrance hall, a section of submarine cable, about fifteen inches long, which sat there together with an assortment of ammonites, trilobites and various other fossil specimens collected by a paleontologically-inclined uncle. The various outer

182

casings of the cable had been progressively removed, like layers of skin, to reveal the tightly packed wire core within. Placed together with the fossils it had a vaguely anatomical feel about in — it could have been the flayed penis of a narwhal or the sectioned tentacle of a giant squid — and like the piece of brontosaurus skin in Bruce Chatwin's grandmother's cabinet, it was an object of queer fascination. This, I was told, was a small part of the telegraph cable which had once traversed the floor of the Indian Ocean and I could imagine it lying there in the darkness of the uncharted depths, passed over by cœlacanths and probed by curious unnamed creatures of the deep, who lit their way with phosphorescent brands dangling at the end of strange protuberances emerging from their heads.

Rodriguez, which was where my grandfather was stationed during the First World War, is situated at 19° 45' S., 63° 25' E., and lies some 365 miles ENE of Mauritius, which in those days was a British colony, having been captured from the French during the Napoleonic wars. My grandfather wrote a book about the island, a mixture of history, geography, ethnography and ecology, which, being the first of its kind, got him elected as an Honorary Fellow of the Royal Geographical Society. Once the home of the dodo and later the haunt of pirates and privateers, Rodriguez was, in my grandfather's time, and still is, a fairly modest sort of place with a mixed population speaking a patois of French Creole (interestingly the latter bears a closer resemblance to the Creole languages of the Caribbean than the French Creole of Rèunion Island 500 miles to the west).

The island is very beautiful, being blessed with crystal-clear streams, fertile soils and a salubrious climate. One of the earliest settlers, François Leugat, fleeing from the French persecution of Huguenots in the late seventeenth century, describes his first impressions:

> We admired the divine and secret workings of Providence which, after suffering us to be ruined and driven from our native country, had extricated us by various marvellous experiences and ordained us at last

to dry our tears in this terrestrial paradise, where we could be rich, free, and happy, and where instead of vain riches we could employ our quiet life to the salvation of our souls.

Even my grandfather, in what is otherwise a fairly dry and academic account of the island, was moved to write, some two and a quarter centuries later:

> Approaching from the sea, Rodriguez presents a very picturesque sight. The long white foamy line made by the incessant rolling of the breakers over the reefs; the deep blue of the ocean, and the brown and green patches of the sea within the reefs, studded with little white sails against the green background of the hills, make an enchanting picture.

The story of how the book came to be written, or at least how I thought the book came to be written, became firmly lodged in my mind during childhood, long before I could point to where Rodriguez was on the map. As related by my mother it was at the beginning of the First World War and my grandfather was one of half-a-dozen cablemen manning the Rodriguez station. One day a battleship was seen on the horizon, steaming towards the island which the cablemen identified as the notorious German light cruiser, *Emden*.

The *Emden*, in the early months of the Great War was the scourge of the Indian Ocean and between August and September 1914 managed to send over 70,000 tons of Allied shipping to the bottom. She also sank the Russian light cruiser *Zhemchug* and a French torpedo boat in Penang Harbour, in broad daylight, before the horrified gaze of the people of George Town, and had previously carried out a similarly daring attack on the oil installations at Madras, which resulted in some 350,000 gallons of fuel going up in smoke. On the 8th October, however, the *Emden's* luck finally ran out and she was surprised by the Australian light cruiser *Sydney* in the Cocos-Keeling Isles, while a raiding party was on shore laying waste to a wireless station on Direction Island. The *Emden* was out-gunned by the Australian ship which had the advantage of superior range and the *Emden*'s captain, Lt. Cmdr. Karl Friedrich Max von Müller, was forced to beach his badly-damaged ship on a reef. Of those on board the *Emden*, 134 lost their lives in the engagement with sixty-five wounded, but the 117 members of her crew who were on shore at the time of the *Sydney*'s attack managed to elude capture and after commandeering a sailing ship — the barquentine *Ayesha* — made their way back to Germany via Jeddah and Istanbul.

But to get back to my grandfather and the cablemen of Rodriguez, their immediate thought upon sighting the *Emden* was to prevent the cable station from falling into enemy hands for if the Germans succeeded in gaining control of the station, then they would be able to tap into top-secret information being sent across the Indian Ocean — unlike wireless signals, which could be intercepted, the submarine cable network provided a watertight means of sending information in times of war. Rodriguez being such an out of the way place and so rarely visited by ships, it might have been months before the Germans were detected, during which time untold damage could have been done to Allied interests in the region, not least by the *Emden* herself. The cablemen therefore decided there and then to trash the cable station and destroy all the records in order to prevent them from falling into enemy hands. Having done so, they found, somewhat to their dismay, that the *Emden* simply steamed past the island and over the horizon into the ocean blue, never to be seen by them again. The cablemen were then obliged to spend several months on Rodriguez before they were relieved and according to my mother, it was during this time that my grandfather, out of boredom with having nothing to do, collected the material for his book which was published as *The Island of Rodriguez: a British Colony in the Mascarenhas Group* in 1923.

A good story and one I have often told, but in carrying out the research for this article, I thought I had better write to my uncle, in the depths of Cornwall to see if he had any further information to add. After reading through my grandfather's papers, he sent back the following reply:

The story from my father relates to an incident in September 1914 at Rodriguez. One afternoon a three-masted iron barque rounded Point Coton and caused quite a stir with the locals as it was unusual for ships to visit. It was flying the French flag in reverse and it anchored off the reef. The magistrate, together with the island's pilot, the corporal and fourteen crew, rowed out to the barque. Alongside they found a local fishing boat without anyone on board and the pilot came to the conclusion that the three men who owned the boat had been taken onto the barque by force.

Peering through the portholes he could see several men with square caps, most of them black but also several whites. Meanwhile a man on the barque, speaking in a very commandeering way invited the magistrate to come aboard, at which point the magistrate grew concerned and told the corporal "They are Germans, let's go."

They got back to Port Mathurin, the principle settlement on the island, at 8.00 P.M. and shortly afterwards the fishing boat arrived back with the three men, who brought with them a letter from the captain of the barque asking for pigs, potatoes, vegetables, fowls and other provisions. The letter was written in very badly worded French and was signed by a Maurice Laborse of the barque *Bonaventure*. Accompanying the letter there was a copy of the *Omar Khayam*, belonging to a P. Hill, with instructions that it should be given to the island's priest (the letter had mentioned that a gift would be sent for the church though it never arrived). One of the fishermen had also been given a shirt, again belonging to P. Hill of Australia, and they reported that while they were on board, they had been asked whether there were any guns on the island and how many English cablemen were there. The captain told them that he would be coming ashore at midnight for his requirements.

On hearing this, the cablemen immediately broke open their armoury, took out their rifles and drew up a plan to defend the station. All the spare cable equipment was hidden and preparations were made to destroy what was in use. It was decided that if the ship's crew made a landing they would be opposed and that if this failed, then guerrilla tactics would be resorted to.

Midnight passed and nothing happened, but at dawn the next day the barque was seen heading for the island. About three miles off she made several small tacks but then set her helm on a course leading away from Rodriguez. The next morning there was no sign of her, but it had been observed from the shore that she was trailing some kind of line from her stern and it was concluded that this was probably an attempt to cut the cable. The barque may have been a prize of the *Emden*.

Clearly a rather different account of what happened to that of my mother's, but an intriguing story nonetheless — I would be interested to learn more about the barque *Bonaventure* and the identity of her mysterious crew. All the same, I have to declare a certain fondness for my mother's somewhat imaginative reconstruction of events, especially the ironic twist at the end when the *Emden* just steams on by, and I suspect that this is the tale that I shall continue to tell at dinner parties in the future. So pass the port and let us "agree to a short armistice with the truth" for the sake of a good story.

DEATH IN MALACCA

*Malacca always seemed to me one of those old places that, having a
kind of half-fabulous antiquity about them — a name and glory
long since faded — are peculiarly attractive to the imagination.*

— An English visitor in 1847 —

In Malacca, a lot of people make a living out of dying. In every street, it seems, there is at least one enterprise given over to the rituals of death. As a child I was always fascinated by the traditional Chinese coffins — huge canoe-like sarcophagi, made from a single tree trunk, with upswept ends which put me in mind of gigantic shoe horns. Two or three of them filled the cramped workshop of the *tukang keranda*, or coffin maker, a thin, balding man in a singlet and a pair of striped boxer shorts, hardly leaving him enough elbow room to work up a French polish on the next in line for the Chinese cemetery on the slopes of Bukit Cina.

And then there were the shops selling Hell money and paper funerary items — a t*owkay's* mansion of matchwood and painted tissue, complete with refrigerators, television sets and the latest model of Mercedes Benz — everything a person might aspire to materially both in this life and, one supposes, the next. I was intrigued by this earthly vision of a life fulfilled beyond the grave and whilst my mother browsed for antiques in a nearby junk shop, I would contemplate the paper riches of the Hereafter.

For many years my father had quite a bit of work in and around the Malacca area. Malayan Fisheries seemed to feature a lot, along with a seaside hotel for Mr. Shah. And then there was an enormous British army camp at Terendah, a little way up the coast which kept him busy for the best part of a decade. This meant that every school holidays there was at least one occasion to motor down from Kuala Lumpur for the day and sometimes an overnight stay. This was a fine thing to do for Malacca, then, was a place set apart from time, sunk in a age-old torpor that had yet to be dispelled by the clamour of the twentieth century. Isabella Bird, the eminent Victorian lady adventurer, describing Malacca in the 1860s wrote of its "mediævalism" where "the noise of the modern world reaches it in only the faintest echoes." Here was a place where one slept "an almost dreamless sleep", while one's waking sensations "seem to come out of books read in childhood". And so it was a hundred years later.

In those days one approached Malacca from Kuala Lumpur across a swathe of verdant *padi* fields. The road ran along the top of a raised dyke, or bund, and to either side was a scene of rural Arcadia stretching to the horizon. Where today the countryside round about has been despoiled by acres of unlovely concrete shophouses and automobile wrecking yards, there were once *kampongs* and orchards. Water buffalo grazed on the stubble of the previous season's rice crop and egrets, white like strips of torn paper, waded in the pools and mires, occasionally hopping on to the back of a passing bovid to feast upon the ticks that infested their mud-caked hides. A line of coconut palms to the west marked the coastline, where the watered rice fields gave way to the sandy beaches and muddy mangroves of the Malacca Straits, while up ahead the twin eminences of Bukit Cina and St. Paul's Hill rose modestly above the roof tops of the ancient town.

Malacca, then, was a small place, hardly bigger than in the days of the Portuguese who encircled it with a wooden stockade. It was the latter which gave rise to the place name Tengkera on the coast road leading north to Port Dickson — the word *tengkera* is a Malay corruption of the Portuguese *tranquerah*, meaning a palisade. As one drew near, a conurbation of *kampong* houses signalled one's imminent arrival and the next instant one was there in the heart of town, a dense lattice of narrow streets, parted by a grey-green greasy Limpopo of a river.

The main thoroughfares, though busy, were less congested with motor vehicles in those days — trishaws were the preferred mode of local transport then — and it seemed that there were a great many more trees, lining the roads or otherwise strategically placed to provide a shady spot where an itinerant *ais kacang* vendor might set up shop. The latter was the local equivalent of a *gelateria* on wheels, serving up heaped shavings of ice, like a fresh fall of snow, studded with a fistful of nuts, beans and other pulses and then liberally dribbled with a stream of brightly coloured syrups —

shocking pink, magenta or an iridescent green were the favoured hues. Even today one can still get stuck into a superior class of *ais kacang* in Malacca.

The first port of call was the old Majestic Hotel, rather ingenuously described as the "Raffles of Malacca." Parking the car under a huge rain tree which in those days shaded the forecourt of that venerable hostelry, my father would make straight for the bar and order an ice-cold beer to refresh himself from the weariness of the road. I would sip more modestly on a fresh lime or else order a *gunah*. The latter beverage, though no longer fashionable, once featured on the bar list of every club and resthouse in the Malay Peninsula, and as it is a first rate way to quench one's thirst on a hot and sticky noonday in the tropics, I shall tell you how it is made.

Quite simple really. Lots of ice in a long glass; ginger ale and ginger beer in equal measures; a few drops of *pahit* (preferably Angostura Bitters); thick slices of orange, lemon and lime; some fresh mint if available (Thai basil will do as an alternative); and lastly, a *glacé* cherry. It can really slake the driest of thirsts and has the feel of an alcoholic drink with none of the evil consequences. The last time I had a *gunah* was with an Elton John roadie at the Sheraton Hotel in Bandar Seri Begawan, four of five years back. In that most arid of 'dry' states, he agreed that the *gunah* could become the drinking man's equivalent of Methadone and a salvation to us all.

The cool drinks slipped easily down welcoming throats and depending on the hour of the day we might sit down to a spot of lunch in the hotel restaurant. Grilled *ikan kurau* — the morning's catch straight off the slab at the wet market — served with freshly quartered limes and crisply fried *pomme frites*: my stomach rumbles just to think of it.

Replete and refreshed we would then go our different ways for the afternoon. My father would drive off to meet his clients whilst my mother headed for the antique shops on Jonkers Street to ruminate amongst the furniture and *bric-à-brac* of past Peranakan lives. I would follow my own path through the old Chinese quarter where strangling figs had rooted themselves in the crumbling stucco, and the faded, weather-worn façades, with their chipped pilasters and broken jalousies, had acquired the pastel hues of an Etruscan fresco.

And through it all wound the river, flowing sluggishly, viscous and opaque, its oily waters occasionally catching the sun in rainbow eddies, carrying the sewerage of the town to the sea. Scrofulous monitor lizards basked on the muddy banks at low tide, oblivious to the prevailing stench of putrefaction and decay, while centuries of discarded rubbish, the broken sherds of history, poked from the slime in a rather sinister fashion, like the poorly-concealed evidence of some nameless crime.

Right beside the hotel there was an old Dutch house, with Tuscan columns and a stoop, standing in a long-neglected and overgrown garden. The roots of the trees had undermined the garden wall which leant drunkenly outwards and a path led up from the rusting wrought-iron gate, which was always locked, to a front door that was always closed. And the shutters too — they were always closed as well, stripped by the elements of their paint, their louvres displaced and set askew. There was something mysterious and captivating about that old place. Did some *nonya* Miss Haversham dwell within, mourning for her *baba* bridegroom amongst dusty brocades and Chinese silks, her table laid with Maastricht and Ming for a wedding feast that never took place? Who knows, but the house and its occupants are gone now and a thirteen-storey medical centre stands on the site.

On the other side of the road from the Majestic, the river looped back on itself and, depending on the tide and time of day, the fishing fleet would be moored there —a cluster of wooden boats with high, wave-breaking prows, and a little cabin at the stern for the crew of nocturnal fishermen who returned with the morning sun, their open holds slithering and sliding like quicksilver with the night's catch.

Kampong Morten stood on the opposite bank — it stands there still, a jumble of traditional Malay houses raised high on pile foundations to escape the inundations of high tide. This is how it came by its curious name. The land, which formerly had been nothing more than a stretch of *nipah* palm and mud on the outskirts of town, was settled in 1921 by the former residents of Kampong Java who were displaced from their homes when a new municipal market was built on the site. They badly needed a riverside location for their new settlement because the men of the community traditionally operated the wooden passenger boats, or *nadeh*, that used to ferry people up and down the river and which also used to meet the steamer that regularly plied between Malacca and Singapore in those days. In the end, the *nadeh* men and their families managed to acquire the present site with the help of a $10,000 loan which was organised for them by a Mr. F. J. Morten, the local collector of land revenue for the government. Later, when they came to choosing a name for their new village, they decided to call it after their benefactor in the colonial administration.

The steamer service between Malacca and Singapore had long been discontinued in the days when I used to visit Malacca with my father, but there was still a man with a *sampan* who provided a ferry service from just in front of the Majestic Hotel to Kampong Morten on the opposite side of the river for a few cents. He wore a conical coolie's hat to shade him from the noonday sun and propelled his craft in the ancient Oriental manner, standing up at the oars and facing the direction in which he was going. Perhaps his father had been one of the *nadeh* owners who originally settled Kampong Morten, back in the twenties. Today, a footbridge spans the river and the last of the Kampong Morten ferrymen has been retired.

A short walk brought one to the foot of St. Paul's Hill, which was once defended by the stout laterite walls of the old Portuguese fort, until the latter was dynamited by the British during the Napoleonic wars. This "most useless piece of gratuitous mischief," as it was later described by Lord Minto, Governor-General of India, was supervised, with many misgivings, by William Farquhar who was later to become the first Resident and Commandant of Singapore. Munshi Abdullah, a native of Malacca and the friend and Malay teacher of Raffles, described how "the gunpowder exploded with a noise like thunder, and pieces of the Fort as large as elephants and even some as large as houses, were blown into the air and cascaded into the sea." "Thus was the beautiful Fort of Malacca utterly annihilated," he sadly commented, adding that "The Fort was the pride of Malacca, and after it destruction the place had lost its glory, like a woman bereaved of her husband, the lustre gone from her face."

Actually, one part of the old fort still stands — the southern gateway, or Porta de Santiago — but only because Raffles himself intervened to prevent its destruction. He was in Malacca in November 1807, recuperating from illness, and wrote to the authorities in Penang agitating for the preservation of the town and what was then left of its fortifications in the interests of posterity and British prestige. The name of Malacca, he argued, "carries more weight to a Malay ear than any new settlement could," and with the place in British hands, "the whole of the Malay rajahs in the Straits and to the Eastward might be rendered not only subservient but if necessary tributary."

And so the Gateway of St. James escaped demolition to become the oldest surviving European structure in this part of the world, its ancient walls mottled with the patina of ages past. One can still make out the Dutch East India Company coat of arms over the portal and the legend *Anno* 1670, the year of its restoration (the fort was badly damaged when the Dutch seized Malacca from the Portuguese in 1641 after a five-month campaign of siege and bombardment).

Behind the Porta de Santiago, a steep path led up to the top of St. Paul's Hill and the roofless ruins of the old church. Today, St. Paul's is something of a tourist trap with a motley crowd of postcard sellers, souvenir touts and vagabonds clustered around the summit, bickering amongst themselves like a covey of disaffected crows. Equally insufferable are the itinerant watercolourists who would like you to pay an absurd sum for their lurid daubs of sunsets and Malay kampongs. And there is also a man who makes novelty key rings; these sort of people one can do without.

Thirty years ago one could climb the hill without a gaggle of school children at one's heels and wander unmolested amongst the tombstones and ruined walls of the old church, soaking up the melancholic atmosphere that inhabited the place. Ancient flame trees cast their shade round about and a sea breeze stirred the long grass which grew between the mouldering graves. I used to go up there with a book and read a bit and think a bit, and then read some more. I liked the old tombstones propped up against the walls of the church. Huge great slabs, as tall as a man, inscribed in Latin, Portuguese and Dutch, and ornamented with images of East Indiamen and Death's heads in relief, memorials to the men of Jan Compagnie, who lay there together with their wives and children. Old stones but such young deaths; half-lived lives claimed by malaria and dysentery, heartbreak and malaise.

And there were English graves, too. An old Protestant cemetery lies at the bottom of the hill with a lichen-covered obelisk, standing in the shade of an ancient mango tree. Here rest the bodies of two Englishmen — Lieutenants James White and E. V. Harding, so the inscription tells us — who lost their lives in the Naning War of 1831-32. The campaign was directed against a fractious Minangkabau Malay element some miles inland who refused to submit to the will of the British government in Malacca and were accordingly subjected to a bit of gunboat diplomacy, albeit at several miles remove from the sea. The war and its causes are long forgotten, but the obelisk stands there still, like a scaled-down version of Cleopatra's needle or some mysterious Mayan stele from the jungle ruins of Chichen Itza.

Back at the top of the hill, within the walls of the ruined St. Paul's, there is a well-like structure with an iron grille across its mouth which is supposedly where St. Francis Xavier was buried, following his death off the coast of China in 1522. He wasn't allowed to rest there in peace for very long, for after six months, his body was exhumed and taken to Goa. Subsequently, in 1614, the mortal remains of St. Francis were again interfered with when the Pope requested that the right arm be severed from the body and sent to Rome. It is said that when the churchmen in Goa came to dismember the Saint, blood gushed forth from the detached limb which rather astonished them, given the fact that St. Francis had been dead for more than sixty years. No less astonishing was the subsequent history of the arm. It is said that when the latter arrived in Rome and was brought before the Pope on a silver platter, il Papa chanced to remark how he wished that the complete St. Francis were there in person, whereupon the severed arm raised itself up and seizing a quill signed "Francis Xavier" on the table.

Curiously, the marble statue of St. Francis Xavier, which stands close by St. Paul's Church, is also missing its right arm, or more accurately, its right hand. Apparently a huge tree fell on the thing sometime after it was placed there in 1953 and when the debris was cleared away the statue was marvelously found to be intact — except for the truncated right arm that is. Zounds!

*

Malacca is a place where the dead and their past are omnipresent — one just can't get away from them. Down in Chinatown there is the mausoleum of Hang Jebat, which was another place I liked to go and visit and reflect upon the terrible injustice of his life. Or death, I should say. Hang Jebat is one of the great heroes of Malaccan history who, together with Hang Tuah and Hang Kasturi, constitute a kind of fifteenth-century Malay counterpart to the Three Musketeers. This is his sad story.

Of the three blood-brothers, Hang Tuah was the Sultan's favourite on account of his many valorous deeds. Other members of the court, however, were jealous of Hang Tuah's success and the special privileges that he enjoyed and so they plotted his downfall, accusing him, quite wrongly, of having an affair with one of the ladies-in-waiting. This alleged misdemeanour on the part of Hang Tuah, so outraged the Sultan that he ordered his immediate execution. However, the Bandahara, or Chief Minister, who knew Hang Tuah to be innocent, took him to a jungle hideaway and then later presented some of his clothing, soaked in goat's blood, to the Sultan, as evidence that the order had been carried out.

Meanwhile, Hang Jebat, who was maddened by the unjust accusations against his friend and comrade, rebelled against the gullible and impetuous Sultan, openly sleeping with his concubines in order to insult him. The Sultan, who was full of remorse at having got rid of the valiant Hang Tuah, bemoaned the fact that he had ordered the latter's execution, saying that he only wished that he could call upon him now to dispose of the noisome Hang Jebat. To the Sultan's great surprise and joy, the Chief Minister revealed Hang Tuah was not dead after all and he was summoned to court to receive a royal pardon.

And so we come to the tragedy — Hang Tuah, after receiving his pardon from the Sultan, was then, to his mortification, ordered to kill his friend Hang Jebat to avenge the Sultan's honour. The princely code of conduct amongst Malay warriors in those days was such that Hang Tuah felt impelled to obey his sovereign lord, even though he was well aware of why his former comrade had behaved so badly. Hang Tuah did, however, allow Hang Jebat a full day's grace to wreak his revenge by running *amok*, the customary rite of protest against an unworthy ruler in traditional Malay society. When the carnage was over, Hang Jebat was krissed to death by Hang Tuah in a final act which left more dead bodies than *Hamlet*.

Was Hang Tuah right to do such a thing? Where should his loyalty have lain — with his friend, or to his sovereign? Was this a case of exemplary service to the Sultan, or was it "Murder most foul"? Five hundred years later, the ironies and injustices still fester.

I still return to Malacca from time to time, but with increasingly mixed feelings. Though the rain tree is no longer there to cast its shade across the threshold, the Majestic Hotel still stands, I'm glad to say, though inevitably the threat of demolition hangs over its head like a perpetually poised sword of Damocles. Sadly the hotel restaurant is long defunct and one must look elsewhere for a plate of *ikan kurau* and chips, but the tea is served in a pot and one can order a round of toast and marmalade for breakfast.

I always ask for room no. 27 on the second floor. It is enormous, with twenty-foot ceilings and huge, shuttered windows that look over a small garden at the side of the building. The walls are painted a faded powder blue, with the doors and windows picked out in silver — actually it looks like someone may have got a job lot of marine antifouling to do the woodwork. The plumbing arrangements are a bit ropy, but you can get a decent hot shower at the end of the day, when twelve hours of solar radiation have warmed the contents of the water tank in the roof to a few degrees below boiling point — too bad, though, if it's been raining.

Meanwhile, downstairs among the potted palms and cane furniture, time passes slowly if indeed it passes at all. Outside, the midday sun may beat down with an eyeball-searing brilliance, but in the crepuscular twilight of the hotel lobby a delicious sense of coolness and tranquillity prevails and one has a notion of what it might be like to be a goldfish at the bottom of a well-appointed aquarium. The ceiling fans whiz round high above one's head, and a senior party rustles his newspaper on the other side of the room. Can thirty years have really passed since I was last here with my father? It would seem so, and my father has been dead for more than half that time, his ashes scattered on a mountainside in Andalusia. So let's have another Tiger Beer and raise a glass to his memory. *Satu empat jalan.*

NO MORE LAND, SAY FISH

Unfading moths, immortal flies,
And the worm that never dies,
And in that heaven of all their wish,
There shall be no more land, say fish.

— Rupert Brooke, 'Heaven' (1915)—

Flying into Changi Airport on a sunny afternoon, one can still catch a glimpse of the occasional *kelong*, or fishing platform, standing in the shallow azure seas that surround our shores. *Kelongs* used to be an important component in the local fishing industry, as familiar a part of the seascape as sailing boats and cumulus clouds. From the land, they looked like rickety oil rigs, silhouetted way out there on the horizon where the sky met the sea, but their daily catch once kept our tables well-provided with a seemingly inexhaustible supply of native fish species. Today, *kelongs* have all but disappeared from the scene, like so many other 'traditional' aspects of the Singaporean economy — fish ponds, poultry farms, pig breeders and market gardens among them. But thinking back a few years, I recall how my father would sometimes organise a weekend on one of these fishing platforms, a little raft of humanity in a watery realm where there was nothing but the boundless sea and the sky, and fish — an ocean full of them.

The typical *kelong* was constructed from *nibong*-palm piles driven deep into the sea-bed on top of which was placed a platform, some 20-30 feet above the waves. A complicated system of stakes in the sea round about lured fish into a netted enclosure at the base of this structure and once the fish were in there, it was almost impossible for them to find their way out. This fish pen was about the size of a badminton court and on the sea bed beneath it lay a second net which could be raised to the surface by a system of ropes attached to each corner. The latter were wound round wooden windlasses with long protruding poles, like the spokes of a capstan, to give extra leverage. Every few hours the fishermen who lived on the *kelong* would man these devices and the net would be slowly hauled up from the bottom, hopefully bringing with it a fine catch of fish. Open boats would come out from the mainland, usually in the early hours of the morning, and the catch would be emptied into them and then shipped off to the dawn fish market on Boat Quay.

It all worked very well and in the past there were literally hundreds of *kelongs* in the shallow seas around Singapore. Some of them were quite substantial structures with *atap* huts that provided accommodation for the fishermen who manned them. The latter worked in alternating shifts, spending a month or more at sea before being replaced by a relief crew.

The *kelong* we used to visit belonged to an 'aunty' of one of the draughtsmen in my father's office and every now and then we would spend the weekend there. Surrounded by sea, without a drawing board or pad of paper to distract him, my father could really relax and get away from it all — in the most literal sense, for this particular *kelong* stood on a sandbank some six miles off shore and there was no land to be seen in any direction.

We would set off from the beach at Bedok in open boats on a Saturday afternoon and it was good to be out on the ocean blue with the great vault of the sky over our heads and huge cumulus clouds hanging on the horizon. Then came the perilous bit when we arrived at the *kelong* and had to disembark, for the boats rose and fell with the waves and one's timing had to be just right as one leapt for the ladder. Once everyone was safely transferred to the *kelong,* the boats returned to the coast and we were there for the night — just the fishermen and ourselves, effectively 'marooned' until the next day on a lonely wooden platform in the middle of the South China Sea — there were, of course, no cell phones in those days, nor was there any other form of communication with the mainland for that matter.

The 'fishing party' usually included one or two members of staff, among them the delectable Sally, my father's secretary, who wore a polka-dot bikini and slept on a Lilo between my parents for fear of the nocturnal attentions of the 'bachelor architects.' There were two of the latter — Colin and Dennis — who could be guaranteed to supply a weekend's entertainment, usually at the expense of the aforementioned Sally who was both excited and terrified by their interest in equal measures.

Life on the *kelong* was basic and we brought our own provisions, which as far as I recollect, consisted of several cases of beer augmented by a couple of bottles of whiskey and an ample supply of smoking materials. We also took some bread and butter, some coffee and milk and some fresh vegetables and rice, but the main course came straight from the sea — an endless stream of *fruit de mer* cooked in a bubbling steam boat or fried in an ancient blackened *wok*.

There was not a great deal to do — mostly we played cards and fished — but just being out there in the midst of the ocean was exciting enough in itself. The light was always changing with the hour of the day and the type of cloud formation, and when night fell the stars were spread over our heads, far brighter than they could ever be on land.

I slept in a corner of a hut with the fishermen, who generally went to bed quite early as they had to get up in the small hours to raise the nets. I can still hear the hissing of the pressure lamp and the low murmur of their voices mingling with the distant chug of a marine diesel — a passing fishing boat heading out to deeper water or else towards a dawn market. At about four o'clock in the morning everyone was roused to join in the raising of the net. It was an exciting moment, with the fishermen straining at the winches, wrapping their arms and legs around the spokes and using the weight of their bodies to rotate the drum through a quarter of a turn at a time. They laboured mightily and it was all they could do to prevent the windlass from spinning madly backwards under the enormous weight of the net and the fish. The ropes attached to the corners of the net were as taut as cat gut and they creaked and groaned as they slipped on the wooden drums around which they wound, but it was a tremendous sight to see the net finally break the surface, the displaced water cascading back into the sea as the night's catch leapt and slithered about like quicksilver in the beam of the flash lights which were turned on this harvest from the deep.

The raising of the net coincided with the arrival of open boats from the mainland, the bottom of their hulls lined with large blocks of ice which would keep the catch fresh until they could be off-loaded at the quayside. The boats rose and fell in the swell, bumping against the barnacled timbers of the *kelong* as they manoeuvred themselves into position to receive the catch. The latter was literally poured into them and secured in place with a stained tarpaulin, whereupon the boats' engines were immediately cranked up and with a shout they were off, heading for the mainland, an hour or more away, in a nightly race to beat the opposition to the market place at dawn — until the 1970s, when the retail fish trade was moved to the new Central Fish Market at Jurong, Boat Quay, just upstream from Coleman bridge, was the place where fresh fish came ashore.

The nightly raising of the nets was certainly an exciting spectacle, but the best moments I recall were the storms. One could see them approaching from afar — a long black cloud on the horizon which rapidly sped towards us across an ominously still and sullen sea, opaque like the sherds of wave-washed glass one finds down by the shoreline. Then the storm would be upon us and the *kelong* would groan and shudder under the combined assault of wind and waves, while the rain and spray would be blown through the flimsy *atap* hut in which we sheltered. At times one felt that the roof might fly off at any moment and the entire *kelong* break up under our feet, which could be a little worrying, but the blow never lasted very long and it was an exhilarating experience to be caught up in a maelstrom of white-capped seas and banshee winds.

On one occasion, however, a storm broke while we were in the boat heading back to the mainland on a Sunday afternoon. Soon there was a large sea running, and we could taste the salt as the wind tore at the crests of the waves and threw them in our faces. We were still a couple of miles from the shore when suddenly, the engine spluttered and died, no doubt flooded by the copious amount of water which was coming over the sides. Unable to keep our bows into the waves, we wallowed in the troughs taking on even more water as the boatman frantically tried to crank his motor back to life. And then, as if able to sense that we were in trouble, two sharks appeared on the scene, their dorsal fins slicing through the gunmetal waters as they circled the boat, Fortunately help was already at hand — another boat in the vicinity had spotted our distress and was coming to our assistance, but not a moment too soon, one felt.

As it happens, in those days it was not uncommon to read of shark stories in the press. For some reason I will always remember one unfortunate Malay fellow who lost a leg while trying to disentangle a fishing line from the propeller of his boat. In my grandfather's day, though, the situation was far worse. This was before proper refrigeration had been introduced to the island and even though the various ice-houses produced enough of the stuff to sink the *Titanic* each day, there was still an awful lot of bad meat to be disposed of on a regular basis. Inevitably, a lot of this rotten meat found its way to the sea and as a consequence the waters off Singapore were nothing short of shark-infested. Indeed, the only way that one could swim in the sea in any safety was if one did so within a specially constructed enclosure called a *pagar*, *pagar* being the Malay term for a fence.

It is very unlikely that one would bump into a shark in the murky seas that break upon our shores today and the *pagar*, like the *kelong*, has become a thing of the past, an historical footnote in the photo library at the National Archives. One consequence is that the fish in our super-markets today are far more likely to have swum in foreign waters than the seas surrounding Singapore; they are the ultimate flying variety, arriving 'jet-fresh' from Thailand or Vietnam, already neatly disembowelled and cleaned for the frying pan or grill. And the proof of this is in the eating, methinks, for *ikan merah, ikan kurau* and *ikan tenggiri* have never again tasted as good as they did in the days of my childhood, when you could guarantee that the fish on your plate had been happily swimming off Tanjong Rhu just the night before. None of this makes much sense to me. Rather, it calls to mind the Woosterish words attributed to the Edwardian architect, Sir Edwin Lutyens, uttered when confronted by an unappetising-looking fish in a restaurant: "This piece of cod passeth all understanding."

ET IN ARCADIA EGO

*The act of vividly recalling the past is something that I seem
to have been performing with the utmost zeal all my life.*

— Valdimir Nabokov, *Speak, Memory* (1967) —

❖

It's a rare thing to live in a house in Singapore these days — the percentage of those who do so must be in single figures — but once upon a time, just about everyone, great and small, lived in house of one sort or another. It might have been an elegant black and white bungalow, or just a simple *kampong* dwelling with an *atap* roof and a long drop at the end of the garden, but it was a house all the same and to my mind, even the latter arrangement would be preferable to a fully-airconned, silent-flushing, everything-with-knobs-on HDB apartment — I like to feel the earth under my feet. But we live in modern times and 'up' is definitely the direction to go. Indeed, one's feet are scarcely allowed to touch the ground, these days, in that it is positively *de rigueur* for the contemporary apartment block to be raised one storey in the air on reinforced concrete piers. One regrettable consequence of this is that it has done away with the vigorous street life that once characterised old Singapore — the rows of shophouses with their merchandise spilling out on to the crowded five-foot way and the *makan* stall with folding chairs and tables tucked around the corner in the alleyway between two terraces. Instead, we have the 'void deck,' which as its name implies is an empty, even desolate, space that only fills up on the occasion of a wedding feast or a wake. All very neat and tidy, of course, but one misses the cheerful, companionable bustle one found on the streets of Chinatown in the old days.

As it happens, the term void deck is doubly appropriate, for one of the meanings of the word void is of course 'to defecate', or 'excrete', which has a particular resonance in a part of the world where houses are symbolically conceived in corporal terms, that is to say, with a 'head', 'body', 'arms' and 'legs.' To elaborate, one often finds that among the Austronesian peoples of South East Asia, the dead make their last exit from the house, not via the front door, which would be inauspicious, but by the back, which in this anthropomorphic scheme of things is typically identified as the 'anus' of the house. Clearly, in the context of a wake, we should recognise the void deck as the symbolic backside of the HDB block — a liminal zone, where one receives one's final discharge from the community and is symbolically 'pooped' out of this world and into the next.

Ultimately, the man responsible for this elevated lifestyle was the French-Swiss Modernist, Le Corbusier, for it was he who first gave us the high-rise apartment dwelling raised on piers, or '*pilotis*' as he called them. And of course, modern-day Singapore, with its serried ranks of functionalist residential units and elevated walkways carrying pedestrians across multi-lane highways, is nothing less than the perfect realisation of Le Corbusier's ideal city of the future. The only thing missing from his vision are the little aeroplanes flying in amongst the tower blocks, which he liked to put in his drawings. I wonder what my grandmother would have thought.

She was born in Singapore in 1894 and had the usual sort of life for those times — being carried around in a palanquin and that kind of thing. The Second World War put an end to all that and by the time I arrived on the scene she had long since departed for England, where she exchanged her gracious colonial lifestyle for a flat over a newspaper shop in Birchington-on-Sea. My main reason for introducing her here is to recall a visit to one of her former homes in Singapore, one rainy afternoon a long, long time ago.

In the early 1920s, my grandmother was newly-married with two small children, and lived in a large single-storey bungalow on Mount Rosie. One day, when I was a child, my mother took me to see the place. The house stood above the road at the top of an embankment and there was a flight of slippery steps carpeted with moss leading up to a level area which had once been the tennis court, but which was now a jungle of cassava and banana trees. The house itself was a little higher up the hill and was derelict and fast becoming a ruin. The rain dripped from the dense undergrowth which surrounded the decaying building and one could almost hear the fungus growing on the spoiled timbers. Brilliant orange lichens stained the mouldering stucco and the clay-tile roof had collapsed in several places. This was the house where my father had lived as a child, my mother told me, and I tried hard to imagine him as a small boy taking lessons with his tutor on the verandah or running down the steps to the tennis court.

Neither my father nor the house in which he lived as a child are still around today, but two of the houses which I grew up in are still standing, which is somewhat astonishing given the extraordinary pace of re-development in the past couple of decades. One of these childhood homes was a largish place on Holland Road and like the house where my father was born, had a tennis court in front of it. I was little more than an embryo then, an infant of a few months' standing, so the first house that I have any real recollection of was at Braddell Heights, which is just off Braddell Road.

Braddell Road was named after Sir Thomas Braddell, Chief Judicial Commissioner of the Federated Malay States (1913-17), who as it happens once proposed marriage to my grandmother. Back in the late fifties and early sixties it was a pleasant country road, shaded by rain trees and bordered by vegetable farms. Fields of *kai lan, pak choi* and *choy sam*, stretched out on either side to a horizon of coconut palms and secondary forest. *Kangkong* and water hyacinth floated in muddy ponds filled with fish, while ducks and geese, immaculate in their white plumage, did gyre and gimble in the wabe. And every so often there was a rambling Chinese farm house or a Malay *kampong*, each surrounded by its own little 'island' of fruit trees and stands of sugar cane and cassava.

The Braddell Heights Estate was an early forerunner of countless subsequent housing developments with overambitious names like Happy Valley Gardens or Lucky Villas. We lived at number one Lynwood Grove, which in those days was as green and leafy a location as the name would seem to imply. Our house was a fairly modest affair — a single-storey bungalow with few architectural pretensions — but it was surrounded by a large garden with a thick hedge of dwarf bamboo. One doesn't see many bamboo hedges today — they harbour snakes, I suppose — but they were

once a common feature of Singaporean gardens. As indeed were snakes, but in those days, when most people lived on the ground and fairly close to nature, they were not a cause for much concern — snakes along with scorpions, hairy caterpillars and other 'nasties' were regarded as part of the natural order of things and pretty much what one would expect if one chose to live on a tropical island.

Python and cobras were the most common species, but I recall a huge krait being discovered once, coiled in the laundry basket, deep in slumber. The latter was dispatched by Ah Jong, our ever-resourceful black and white Cantonese *amah*, who deftly inserted a broom handle through its coils and slung the still somnolent serpent through an open window. As I have said, snakes did not worry us unduly and we were not inclined to kill them for just being there.

The garden was my natural domain and I was intimate with every corner of it. A lofty flame of the forest grew at one end while behind the house there were fruit trees — mango, pomelo, *rambutan* and *belimbing* ('star fruit') — which were more successfully harvested by the Prevost's squirrels, who kept an attentive eye on their fruiting seasons, than ourselves. A steep, almost vertical, embankment at the end of the garden to the rear of the house was home to a large number of toads who lived in deep holes set in the side of this earth escarpment. At dusk they would come to the mouth of their burrows to gulp in the evening air and an occasional passing insect on the wing.

At the top of this bank lay another area of level lawn densely infiltrated by 'sensitive plants', whose delicate bipinnate leaves folded together when touched. This was a good place to fly kites on a windy day. Speaking of which, on the other side of the road from our house was a *kampong* where there lived a celebrated master kite maker whose fabulous creations of wicker, paste and coloured paper often came to grief in the flame of the forest at the bottom of our garden. He had a particular liking for kites in the shape of animals and people. A shadow would flit across the lawn and looking up one would see a huge figure soaring a couple of hundred feet in the air above one's head. One of his more fantastic creations was a larger than life-size couple, holding hands. They too ended up in shreds in the flame of the forest, becoming forever identified in my mind as "the man all tattered and torn," haplessly stranded in the treetops with his sweetheart, "the maiden all forlorn."

The *kampong* across the road stood amongst a grove of coconut trees and was a fairly 'mixed' community, with Malays, Indians and Chinese all living, if not side by side, then at least in close proximity with one another. The master kite maker was definitely a Malay — the man all tattered and torn was togged out in a *sarong* and *songkok* — but there were dogs and pigs running around, which were treated with ecumenical indifference.

I was personally fascinated by the pigs, which seemed to be unnaturally long, like stretched limousines, with great sagging bellies that dragged in the dirt as they ponderously shuffled from one salubrious rooting spot to another. And of course there was always a great number of squealing piglets, running tight-arsed here and there, head-butting their over-extended mothers in their enthusiastic attempts to attach themselves to a pendulous teat. Every so often the little ones would be rounded up and roughly pushed into loosely-woven wicker baskets, to be slung unceremoniously on the back of a lorry and then driven off to market. The odd half-hour that it took to accomplish this was a desperate time as the terrified little porkers shrieked their hearts out in their rage and anguish at being separated from their mothers; I was happy not to be around on market days.

But pigs and kite flying were not the only entertainments that the *kampong* had to offer. The most spectacular event that comes to mind was an eclipse of the moon. I remember waking in the middle of the night to the din of drums and crashing cymbals, accompanied by a chorus of yells and whistles, as the entire village turned out to scare off the dragon that was traditionally said to be swallowing the moon. Anyone who could lay their hands on something to bash or beat, did so — I was provided with a cake tin and ladle — and together we chased the moon-eating monster from the skies.

Chinese New Year was another time of noise and confusion as firecrackers shattered the peace for four days and nights, without cease. Sleep was only possible with plugged ears, if at all, and the dog and the cats were scared witless. Literally hundreds, maybe even thousands, of firecrackers would be rigged up in series, so that they would self-ignite, one after another, the chain of quick-fire explosions passing back and forth along great festoons of these bangers, slung between the trees and houses of the *kampong*. The effect was like a continuous burst of machine gun fire lasting several minutes and was no less devastating as neighbour competed with neighbour for the dubious distinction of having sponsored the noisiest and lengthiest pyrotechnic display of the festivities. I loved the sulphurous smell of gunpowder as clouds of smoke billowed across the road after one of these explosive extravaganzas. By the end of Chinese New Year, the village lay under a thick carpet of vermilion firecracker paper which covered the ground like fallen chestnut blossom. There then followed a great silence — the eerie hush of an armistice — which heralded the dawn of the fifth day of the new year. The dogs had barked themselves hoarse and the song birds had all flown away; not even the village roosters crowed on the morn that followed the conclusion of this mind-numbing annual cacophony.

Normally, though, one did awake to a dawn chorus of garden birds and crowing cockerels and whenever I hear the morning cackle of a cock today, I am immediately transported back to my early childhood, where it is forever eight o'clock on a brilliant tropical morning, the garden suffused in a warm sunlight that has yet to burn off the heavy dew that glistens on lawn and leaf and spangles the spider's web with sparkling drops of moisture. *Et in Arcadia ego.*

There were, of course, less clement days when dark storm clouds would foregather behind the coconut palms whose fronds would soon be thrashing wildly as the wind that brought the rain swept through them. *Amahs* in neighbouring houses would call to one another across the hedgerows to warn of the impending deluge — 'Ah Jong-ah, *ujan!*' — and everyone would rush outside to gather in the laundry as the first huge drops of rain, big as 50-cent pieces, splashed down.

I always thrilled to the prospect of a good tropical monsoon downpour, with its deluvian release of water accompanied by terrifying discharges of electricity and thunderous uproar. On one occasion the wireless set received a direct hit — Cliff Richard went off the air with a sizzling crack as the room was lit up with the brilliance of a magnesium flare. And then there was just the sound of falling rain, a curl of smoke rising from a few sherds of plastic, and a strong whiff of charred Bakelite hanging in the air.

At these elemental times, Ah Jong would retire to her room, together with the dog and the cats, and sit herself down on the edge of her bed with her hands over her ears to block out the peals of thunder. Sometimes she would wind one of my father's old singlets around her head for good measure, while the cats flattened themselves to the ground beneath her bed. My mother, who had once been struck by lightning in Haifa, always put on a pair of rubber flip-flops — she said that the rubber soles would insulate her from the ground, but I don't know how effective this measure might have been as she was never struck by lightning again.

After the storm had passed, the ground would be strewn with palm fronds and broken branches, and the air would be fresh and cool and scented with the warm sweet smell of the wet earth. Darwin once observed that there is nothing so evocative as the half-remembered smell, and should I go into the garden today, after a heavy downpour, I can, in an instant, step back forty years into the garden of my childhood.

Sometimes, there would be a light shower while the sun was still shining and on these occasions I would run around the garden in my shorts, leaping and dancing in the warm wet rain like a crazed Gymnosophist. Once, I remember, it poured down on one side of the house but not on the other. This extraordinary state of affairs persisted for several minutes — the air must have been especially still — and I was delighted by the simultaneous experience of sunshine and rain at opposite ends of the garden.

Rain was not always welcome, though, for it could bring disaster to the 'brickworks.' I was much given to making little bricks and clay plaques, decorated with fish designs in relief, from natural clay deposits in the garden, which I would leave to bake on the concrete apron surrounding the house. A surprise shower could wash away a day's work.

Other outdoor interests included watching the bonfire. Sucaratnam, the Tamil gardener, could keep a bonfire smouldering for days by continually adding damp leaves and wet grass on top and round the sides and not allowing the glowing interior to burst into flames. My job was that of 'fire-watcher' — I had to let him know if I saw any flames licking through from the red-hot core of the fire, whereupon 'Sugar Rat' — I could never get my child's tongue around his polysyllabic name — would damp down the spot with more wet leaves and grass cuttings. At the end of a couple of days, when all the garden refuse had been consumed in this way, we were left with a huge smouldering cone of ash, which naturally I identified as a volcano, having once accompanied my parents to the top of Mount Vesuvius. Each time, the volcano was recreated anew and in my imagination, I would scale myself down to the size of Tom Thumb and traverse their powdery slopes like a latter-day Pliny, though with less fatal consequences.

When he wasn't tending to the garden, old Sugar Rat would squat in the shade by the side of the driveway with a fearsome array of sickles, *parangs* and other sharp implements beside him. These he would hone on a whetstone, pausing from time to time to wipe the blade with an oily rag. The noise of metal sliding over stone and the swish of dead leaves being swept up with a stiff broom, both belong to a vocabulary of sounds which can instantly conjure up a time long past but happily recalled.

At the risk of seeming to state the obvious, I would say that childhood is a critical period in any person's life. I don't mean this in the commonplace sense that the child is father to the man, but rather that if one's early years have been miserable or deprived, then it is often the case that in adult life one tries to distance oneself from them as much in physical terms as in any other way. Conversely, if one has been blessed with a happy childhood, full of sunshine and light, the opposite is true and one finds oneself in later life, trying to recreate the landscape that first gave shape to those early pleasures. Certainly, the latter is true for me, for although Singapore in the twenty-first century is hugely different to the Singapore of my childhood, nevertheless when I am at home and looking out from my studio window across the sun-dappled lawn and Heliconia beds into the cool shadows of the orchard behind my house, I experience a certain sense of 'belonging' and, equally, a sense of a continuity with the past.

Ultimately, I think the garden has a lot to do with it. When I was a child, my father sometimes took his local leave at Fraser's Hill, in the central highlands of Malaysia, where the air was fresh and cool, and the climate that of a perpetual summer's day. The holiday always included a visit to the dairy farm where I would be forced to quaff down pints of fresh milk, which was not readily available in Singapore in those days. The cows had a certain bovine charm to them, I had to admit, but I hated drinking the beastly stuff, and would have much rather added a drop of sweetened condensed milk to my tea than the real thing. I shall always remember, though, an ornamental garden close by to the dairy farm where there grew all kinds of exotic blooms — 'English flowers' my mother called them — roses, gladioli, marigolds and the like. There, in amongst the blossom and the foliage was a little stone fountain, or it might have been a bird bath, with the following verse engraved upon it:

> *The kiss of sun for pardon,*
> *The song of birds for mirth,*
> *One is nearer God's heart in a garden,*
> *Than anywhere else on Earth.*

Of course these words can be found, repeated a hundred thousand times and more, on bird baths and fountains the length and breadth of the British Isles, though I didn't know it then. For me, however, they still retain a particular poignancy for having been encountered first in a shady corner of that long-forgotten garden in Malaya all those years ago. The sentiments are those of Dorothy Frances Gurney (1850-1932), so my *Dictionary of Quotations* tells me, and to modern ears they sound distinctly hackneyed, even slightly risible, for ours is a cynical and irreligious age. But I didn't think so then, and mine is the loss if I should think so now.

GLOSSARY

Note: the letter 'c' in Malay is pronounced 'ch' as in chocolate.

ais kacang	(Malay) ice shavings and beans, served with a sticky syrup.
ama	(Portuguese) nurse.
amah	(Chinese?) female, domestic household servant.
ang mo	(Hokkien) lit. 'red devil'; (derogatory) term for a European.
antefix	(architecture) an ornamental fixture above a cornice.
atap	(Malay) palm-leaf thatch used in Malay vernacular architecture.
ayer	(Malay) water.
baba	(Straits Malay) Straits-born Chinese male, usually from Malacca and often with some degree of Malay parentage – see Peranakan.
balacan	(Malay) spicy prawn and chilli paste.
balek rumah	(Malay) to return to one's house.
belimbing	(Malay) star fruit (*Averrhoea carambola*).
briani	(Hindi) Indian saffron rice, flavoured with cardamon, cinnamon and cloves, and served with meat curry.
choy sam	(Chinese) spinach mustard (*Brassica para-chinensis*).
chummery	(Anglo-Indian) a mess – shared accommodation for bachelors.
durian	(Malay) the celebrated fruit of *Durio zibethinus* and related species.
ECP	East Coast Parkway – one of Singapore's major arterial motorways.
empat	(Malay) four.
es manis	(Malay) lit. 'sweet ice'; an ice lolly.
hantu	(Malay) a ghost, spirit or sprite.
hantu belian	(Malay) tiger spirit,
HDB	Housing Development Board – Singapore Government public housing body responsible for providing low-cost accommodation.
ikan bilis	(Malay) anchovies (usually sun-dried).
jalan	(Malay) road, path, way, course.
kacang	(Malay) generic name for beans.
kai lan	(Chinese) Chinese kale (*Brassica oleracea alboglabra*).
kampong	(Malay) hamlet, village; a cluster or aggregation of things.

kangkong	(Chinese) water convolvulus (*Ipomea acquatica*).
KL	Kuala Lumpur.
kuey teow	(Chinese) fried rice noodles with added prawns, clams and sausage.
kongsi	(Chinese) a Chinese association or society, often based on clan or guild affiliations.
kopi tiam	(Malay) old-style coffee shop or café.
kolek	(Malay) a type of Malay sailing boat, traditionally used for racing.
lalang	(Malay) a type of coarse grass (*Imperata spp.*).
mah jong	(Chinese) a game rather like a card game only played with tiles with suits and hands – usually played for monetary stakes.
makan	(Malay) to eat; food.
makan angin	(Malay) lit. 'to eat the wind'; to go for a stroll, to make a promenade.
mamak	(Sanskrit) 'uncle', polite form of address for senior Indians; *mamak* stall – Indian 'corner shop' selling cigarettes, newspapers, sweets, etc.
mata-mata	(Malay) lit. 'eyes'; local slang for the police.
mee goreng	(Chinese/Malay) fried noodles with added bits and pieces.
mem	(English/Hindustani) a contraction of 'madam sahib'; a polite term of address for European women in Singapore and Malaysia; still used in shops and restaurants today.
minum	(Malay) a drink; to drink.
MRT	Mass Rapid Transportation – Singapore's passenger railway service.
mui tsai	(Chinese) lit. 'little younger sister'; term used for a maid often sold into service by her parents or an abductor.
nai ma	(Chinese) wet nurse.
naga	(Southeast Asia) mythical serpent.
Nanyang	(Chinese) 'Southern Ocean'; the traditional Chinese toponym for maritime South East Asia.
nadeh	(Malacca Malay) ferry man.
nasi goreng	(Malay) fried rice with added bits and pieces.
nasi lemak	(Malay) rice cooked in coconut milk.
nipah	(Malay) indigenous palm species (*Nipa fructicans*).
nonya	(Straits Malay) Straits-born Chinese female, usually from Malacca and often with some degree of Malay parentage – see Peranakan.
Orang Asli	(Malay) collective term for the various aboriginal (non-Malay) peoples of the Malay Peninsula.

Glossary

Orang Laut	(Malay) lit. 'Sea People', nomadic sea gypsies, etc.
orang putih	(Malay) lit. 'white man'; Europeans and other Caucasians.
P&O	Peninsular & Oriental Steamship Company, established 1840.
pagar	(Malay) fence or palisade.
pahit	(Malay) bitter, as in gin *pahit*, 'gin and bitters'.
pak choi	(Chinese) celery cabbage (*Brassica rapa chinensis*).
pandan	(Malay) screwpine and other members of the genus Pandanus.
parang	(Malay) machete-like chopper.
pawang	(Malay) shaman, a man who employs magical skills.
Peranakan	(Malay) 'native-born' Straits Chinese, usually with some Malay blood, who, in the course of several generations, have adopted many Malay customs and speak a mixture of Malay and Chinese.
Penarik Beca	(Malay) *Trishaw Rider* – a Malay film starring the actor P. Ramlee.
popiah	(Chinese) a type of spring roll.
porte cochère	(French) covered porch to shelter passengers alighting from carriages.
prahu	(Malay) boat – typically a wooden sailing vessel, bigger than a *sampan* but smaller than a ship (*kapal*).
rambutan	(Malay) a fruit a bit like a lychee (*Nephelium lappaceum*).
rendang	(Malay) baked or fried; a meat sauce made with tamarind.
roti paratha, roti canai	(Hindi) a type of Indian bread eaten with *dhal* or curry; sometimes called "Singapore's answer to the croissant."
samfu	(Chinese) woman's blouse with frog buttons and a Mandarin collar.
sampan	(Chinese) generic name for smallish, flat-bottomed boats.
sayur lodeh	(Malay) mixed vegetable stew flavoured with cassava leaves.
SIT	Singapore Improvement Trust, colonial forerunner of HDB.
stengah	(Malay) 'half' (*satu tengah*)
teh tarik	(Malay) 'drawn tea' – frothy tea poured from a considerable height from one glass into another, several times over; a local 'cappuccino.'
towkay	(Chinese) proprietor, store owner, boss-man.
tuan	(Malay) 'sir' or 'mister'; a polite term of address for persons of rank, ubiquitously applied to European men (*orang putih*) throughout the East Indies until a few years ago.
twakow	(Chinese) wide-beamed, flat-bottomed barge propelled by oar, with a sail for use in the harbour and coastal waters.
ujan	(Malay) rain.

CAPTIONS AND PICTURE CREDITS

1   Taking tea at the races, 1920s (Antiques of the Orient, Singapore [AOTO]).

5   Bank of China, Raffles Hotel and Boat Quay in the mid-1950s (JD).

9   JD with Wong Ah Jong, 1960 (JD).

21   Chinese junk off Collyer Quay, 1948 (K. F. Wong/National Archives).

31   Malayan Airways DC3 at Kallang Airport (National Archives).

35   Qantas Empire Airways, Paya Lebar Airport (National Archives).

43   The duffle coat at Manston Airport, Kent, 1961 (JD).

45   Tiger hunt, Choa Chu Kang, 1928 (National Archives).

61   Singapore Botanic Gardens (AOTO).

75   East Coast, mid-1950s (National Archives).

82   Beach near Changi, c. 1957 (JD).

87   Ponggol, with Pulau Ubin in the background, c.1958 (JD).

89   Black and white bungalow, Seton Close (JD).

98   The Corbusian villa, Newton Road, 1959 (JD).

103   Marble Hill Cutting, north of Ipoh, 1890s (AOTO).

115   Jungle road, Malaya (AOTO).

119   Galpins House and the Norman Staircase, King's School Canterbury (JD).

127   Kallang Airfield on fire after a Japanese air raid, with Rochor Canal in the foreground, February 1942 (Australian War Memorial).

143   Postcard sent from on board the M.S. Willem Ruys, May 1956 (JD).

155   Port Swettenham, October 1958 (JD).

157   Convalescence Bungalow, Fraser's Hill, 1960 (JD).

173   Dust-jacket from *The Island of Rodriguez*, by A. J. Bertuchi (1923) (JD).

187   The mail boat puts in to Rodriguez during the First World War (JD).

189   Funerary offerings and paper mannequins, Malacca 1993 (Helen West).

196   Porta da Santiago, Malacca (AOTO).

201   Majestic Hotel, Malacca (JD).

203   Fishing drying (JD).

211   Al fresco bathing at Lynwood Grove (JD).

216   No.1 Lynwood Grove; taking tea on the verandah; talking to Oedipus the cat, with the *kampong* in the background; Hamish the dog (JD).

220   AMD with Hamish the dog, 1959 (JD).

229   With Hamish the dog, Lynwood Grove (JD).

–   Back cover photo (Shivani Mehta).